Please Return To: Karrie Tracy
(307) 202-1700

Redeeming Creation

The Biblical Basis for Environmental Stewardship

FRED VAN DYKE
DAVID C. MAHAN
JOSEPH K. SHELDON
RAYMOND H. BRAND

FOREWORD BY
JAMES W. SIRE

InterVarsity Press
Downers Grove, Illinois

InterVarsity Press
P.O. Box 1400
Downers Grove, IL 60515
World Wide Web: www.ivpress.com
E-mail: mail@ivpress.com

InterVarsity Press® is the book-publishing division of InterVarsity Christian Fellowship®, a student movement active on campus at hundreds of universities, colleges and schools of nursing in the United States of America, and a member movement of the International Fellowship of Evangelical Students. For information about local and regional activities, write Public Relations Dept., InterVarsity Christian Fellowship, 6400 Schroeder Rd., P.O. Box 7895, Madison, WI 53707-7895.

Cover photograph: Jacques Jangoux/Tony Stone Images

ISBN 0-8308-1872-3

Printed in the United States of America ∞

Library of Congress Cataloging-in-Publication Data

Van Dyke, Fred.
  Redeeming creation: the Biblical basis for environmental
stewardship/Fred Van Dyke . . . [et al.].
      p.   cm.
  Includes bibliographical references and index.
  ISBN 0-8308-1872-3 (pbk.: alk. paper)
  1. Environmental protection—Religious aspects—Christianity.
2. Human ecology—Religious aspects—Christianity.   3. Environmental
ethics.   I. Title.
  BT695.5.V36   1996
  261.8'362—dc20   *95-26744*
                                                                          CIP

21   20   19   18   17   16   15   14   13   12   11   10   9   8   7   6   5

15   14   13   12   11   10   09   08   07   06   05   04   03   02

Foreword

"Blah, blah, blah . . ." So chanted a small group of street actors at the edge of the dais from which I was speaking. Fortunately we were outside and I had the microphone. The "blah, blah, blah" was muted. Only I could hear. But why the chant?

The date was Earth Day, 1990; the place, the quadrangle of the main campus of the University of Minnesota. There I was at an open microphone, given fifteen minutes to address students between classes. My topic was "Ecological Responsibility: A Christian Approach." My sponsors were several Christian groups who wanted to explain why Christianity provided a firm basis for environmental ethics.

Presumably the actors and I were on the same side. We were all there to promote concern for the environment. Yet obviously they were not there to support what I was saying. But why?

I can guess. In 1967 Lynn White in his essay "The Historical Roots of the Ecological Crisis" laid the responsibility for the crisis squarely on the shoulders of Christians and what he took to be the biblical view of nature. A case can certainly be made that Christians bear a major responsibility for our ecological crisis. But the fault is not their biblical but their unbiblical view of nature. Christians have long failed to understand what the Bible really teaches concerning nature and our responsibility for it. For this there is no excuse. Repentance must be our first response.

Our second response must then be to right the wrongs of our faulty understanding and act accordingly. We are responsible to know what can be known of God's will for nature, and we are then responsible to act on that knowledge.

This book is an excellent place to start. Though the authors make no claim to be theologians, they have caught the spirit of God's intentions for nature far better than many if not most professional theologians. What is at least as impressive about this book is the eloquence of its presentation. The exposition is seasoned with stories of the authors' own engagement with nature. Don't miss the story of the peepers in chapter six! Throughout the text, style and content combine to lead the reader not just to understand nature but to worship its Creator.

Worship is, in fact, the first of a number of practical applications the authors call for in the closing pages of the book. The argument, however, begins with theology, moves to ethics and ends in application.

Never far from their attention are the multiple environmental problems we face today: population explosion, air and water pollution, desertification, depleting rainforests, destruction of animal habitats, the death of entire species, depleting ozone layer and global warming. The facts are not exaggerated either to inspire fear or to so overwhelm as to serve only as a counsel of despair. Rather, in the light of Scripture and the presence of God these crises can be faced in hope. The authors' practical suggestions for individuals, families and the larger Christian community are wise and judicious.

I wish, in fact, my father could have read this book. He was a farmer and rancher, and for seven years the county agent in Boyd County, Nebraska. He was a conservationist—but only from the perspective of land use. One day I asked him why the new bridge across the Niobrara River had been built several hundred yards downstream and the road diverted from its former route. "Oh, some *radical* [always a bad word for Dad] environmentalists made a fuss and got the ear of the state highway commission. They diverted the road so as not to disturb a tiny wetland. That road should have gone right straight across the river."

Well, Dad, this book is a little late for you. And it probably will not be read by the street actors at the University of Minnesota. But it should be. This is not a book just for Christian environmentalists. It should be read by every Christian who wants to be a simple disciple of Christ.

James W. Sire

Preface

"The earth is the LORD's, and everything in it," wrote the psalmist (Psalm 24:1). But the cedars of Lebanon, which were a part of the earth the psalmist knew, are gone.

"The heavens declare the glory of God; the skies proclaim the work of his hands" (Psalm 19:1). But today in many parts of the world what the sky proclaims is dimmed and muted by a yellow-brown haze, and scars on the earth below testify to its own erosion.

"God saw all that he had made, and it was very good" (Genesis 1:31). But today many of God's good creatures are threatened, endangered and disappearing from the earth forever.

This book is about redeeming creation. Originally it was conceived as part of our work as members of a working group called the Global Resources and Environment Commission (GRAEC), established by the American Scientific Affiliation (ASA). The ASA is a fellowship of some twenty-five hundred Christians (members and subscribers) engaged professionally in the practice, study and teaching of science and committed to understanding the relationship of science to the Christian faith in service to the church and the scientific community. Within that

mission, our commission's purpose was to address current environmental issues and problems within an understanding of Christian faith,
and to bring to those problems genuine ethical solutions within a
biblical perspective.

For too long many people in their sacred assemblies have acknowledged God as Creator but failed to care for the creation he made.
Others have erred in worshiping the creation rather than the Creator,
replacing God with something less. The goal of this book is to reveal
the joy and beauty of the world around us, with humanity's rightful
responsibilities for its care, through an understanding of who God is
to us as Creator, what the world is as his creation and what we humans
are as the creatures who alone are made in his image. Along with the
development of biblical answers to these questions, we present an
overview of the current ecologic crisis and the biblical principles that
should guide our responses to it.

But none of this is exceptionally original, at least on the surface. In
recent years there have been a number of books on the relationship
between ecology and Christianity. A fair and obvious question is, Why
another one?

Having reviewed a long list of titles on the subject of Christianity and
ecology, we have read many books by ecologists who, though Christians,
did not seem to have a clear grip on the relation of their faith, or of
biblical thought, to the ecological problems they so earnestly and
professionally addressed. On the other hand, we have read books by
theologians who demonstrated great sophistication in handling biblical knowledge and doctrine, but who lacked both knowledge and
experience in linking these ideas to the realities of God's created order.
We have read books expressly written for "ordinary people" that so
oversimplified both Christian faith and ecology as to render their
connection superfluous. At the other extreme, we have perused works
of great intellectual content which, unfortunately, were almost unread-
able to all but a small circle of specialized scholars.

When all was read and done, we concluded that a need still existed—
a need for a book at once readable and serious, a book that would not
reduce three-dimensional problems to two-dimensional homilies or
issues of depth to talk-show shallowness. At the same time we desired
to write *well*, for it is a *story* we offer to our readers, not a research report.

To combine such qualities in one book is, to say the least, difficult. We do not presume to have succeeded, but we are not ashamed to say that has been our aim. The reader will judge our skill and our success.

We are laymen, not theologians, but we are also scientists and teachers within the evangelical Christian community. We relate regularly with theologians (and, more important, with our own students) to demonstrate theological truth as living and practiced reality. To this end we have not only summarized facts but been willing to tell stories—stories of life and experience. In telling these stories, we have tried to demonstrate that the subjects we write about are not merely ideas in our heads but practices in our lives. They are practices of faith, reflecting our commitment as believing Christians, and practices of our work as professional scientists and teachers. We have decided, deliberately, not to identify which of us is the source of any particular story. We ask the reader to treat the stories, like the book, as part of a collective consciousness of our combined experience.

The recognition of our role as stewards is the road back to the obedience of God's command to "tend the garden." There are many ways this restoration can begin. Creation's final redemption awaits the return of our Creator. But our actions today can reveal our reverence and obedience to the God who will accomplish that redemption and upholds creation by the word of his power.

To encourage this obedience in ourselves and our readers, we have risked stating not ideas only but, where appropriate, our passions and sentiments as well. We have done this because we are convinced that correct thinking wedded to right sentiment forges conviction that has the power to change environment and life.

Given this view, the reader will find some of our statements "controversial." We could not avoid it. We only pray that whatever controversies and discussion the book may foster, they will lead ultimately to the attention and glory of our Master, Jesus Christ, and to the substantial healing of his creation. We confess that we love both. And we confess that we have come to know God not only as Savior but also as Creator. May all our readers come to share the joy this knowledge brings, and celebrate freely the life of creation around us.

1
A Creation in Crisis

I found everywhere the wisdom and
goodness of the Creator: but too seldom saw
any inclination among men to make
use of them.
P E T E R   K A L M [1]

I WALKED SLOWLY THROUGH THE ROCK-STREWN RAVINE, HOPPING from one to another of the square black rocks that littered its floor. A stream meandered among the stones, patiently seeking a path to lower ground. A flash flood had filled this ravine several days before. But now all was dry, save for the stream and scattered pools of water among the rocks. Peering over the edge of a boulder in front of me, I spied a common but seldom seen creature, a long-tailed weasel. So intent was he in staring at whatever lay on the other side of the stone that I went unnoticed. Slowly and quietly I moved behind him, closer with each step, to see what he studied. I was within a few feet of him when, suddenly, looking up, he saw me and bolted across the rocky ravine to the trees of the concealing forest on the other side.

I took his perch on the stone and looked down. Nestled in the rocks below lay a pool of water, perhaps two feet deep and three feet wide. In it rested some half-dozen six- to eight-inch rainbow trout. Washed from their home in the nearby stream by the flood of several days before, they waited, trapped like the proverbial fish in a barrel. I wondered, as I looked, what schemes the little weasel must have contemplated to turn a fish in the pool into a fish in the paw.

That weasel and I parted company in southern Utah many years ago. Yet I still remember him, for his contemplations were not so very different from mine. How can we make a living taking limited resources from a shrinking environment, and what about tomorrow? The weasel, like me, was considering the problem of resource management and extraction.

Today our planet faces an environmental crisis wrought by the ever-increasing demands and changes of its human population. Ironically it is this same humanity which God designated to care for the earth, not to destroy it. Yet humans have become a modern-day example of a fox (or perhaps a weasel) put in charge of the hen house. Our interests have been self-centered.

The Bible provides clear and principled instruction, with compelling vision, of what God's creation means to him and what it ought to mean to us. This book is our attempt to present both the instruction and the vision of the Bible's message regarding our responsibility to care for the earth and its inhabitants. Personally and corporately, as individuals and as communities, Christians will add significant dimensions to their life and witness in the world as they discover both the joy and service involved in God's plan for a redeemed creation.

Troubling Questions, Troublesome Doubts

Frank Graham Jr., in his book *The Adirondack Park*, recalls a story told by J. B. Harrison of the American Forestry Congress. Harrison rode one day through the Adirondack Mountains of New York with a prominent lumberman. "We traveled all day," recalls Harrison, "through a blighted and hopeless land. As league after league of utter desolation unrolled before us, we became more and more silent. At last my companion exclaimed, 'This whole country's gone to the devil, hasn't it?' I asked what was, more than anything else, the reason or cause of it. After long thought he replied, 'It all comes to this—it was because there was nobody to think about it, or to do anything about it. We were all busy, and all somewhat to blame. But it was a large matter, and needed the cooperation of many men, and there was no opening, no place to begin a new order of things here. I could do nothing alone, and there was nobody to set us to work together on a plan to have things better; nobody to represent the common object.' "[2]

This "common object" to which Harrison's companion refers is the world around us, the creation of God. When we begin at the beginning, the correct order is God, the heavens, the earth, various life forms and humans. The focus of this book is based on the truth that "God made the earth by his power; he founded the world by his wisdom" (Jeremiah 10:12). Our Creator has seen fit to delegate to humans a limited authority to care for his creation. Thus, our physical environment must be understood in relation to the revelation of God in Scripture. And one of the central teachings of this revelation is that the natural world is not at all natural. It is the creation of a supernatural God. What we routinely call "nature" is in fact "creation." The world around us is the result of God's direct and indirect activity, though it can be (and is) modified by humans.

Christians view the world in this way because they believe in a Creator, and have held this belief ever since they were first called Christians at Antioch. Even before that, the Israelites worshiped the God of Abraham, Isaac and Jacob as the One who had put the stars in place. Today in our world the Scriptures continue to provide abundant evidence that the God of the Bible still desires that humans care for the earth. The pervasiveness of environmental degradation in our day bears witness to the need for this care.

Two basic statements summarize this Christian viewpoint: (1) God is the Creator and Sustainer of our world and (2) God has given human beings the privilege and responsibility of carefully managing it. As have many theologians, philosophers and church fathers of old, the scientist-authors of this book affirm the belief that there is a purpose and meaning to the universe and all that it contains. It is not the product of chance. In the beginning God took the initiative and through Jesus Christ created all things (John 1:3). In all of recorded history there is no more majestic statement than "In the beginning God created the heavens and the earth" (Genesis 1:1). But even more significant than this statement's historical and literary quality is the reality of its truth.

But once acknowledged, what are the consequences and implications of God's creation of the earth and of our management of it? The Bible says that "even the demons believe that—and shudder" (James 2:19). Do we also believe and do nothing? Or is it not incumbent upon us to revere and respect the created world, to help preserve its wildlife and to avoid contaminating its soil, water and air? Is there not a sense in which we should remove our sandals, as Moses did in the desert, because the ground is holy if God is there? Let us proclaim it again and unmistakably. God was there, and God is here today. Not only that, but he has given us the tasks as descendants of Adam to care for his beautiful and intricate creation.

God the Sustainer

God has not left creation merely to fend for itself. With few exceptions, the church has paid much attention to God the Creator but little attention to God the Sustainer. Is not human creativity that results in scientific discovery, musical composition or artistic excellence remembered and cherished?

Throughout its pages, the Bible reveals a God who displays a continuing and constant interest, control and relation to his creation. But what does God see in the world today?

The Environment Today

In 1950, world population was approximately 2.5 billion humans.[3] On July 11, 1987, tiny Matej Gasper, a baby born in what was then the nation of Yugoslavia, was proclaimed the world's five billionth citizen.[4] Before the year 1997 more than six billion people are expected to share this planet.[5]

Daily shifts are occurring in this world human population which will strongly affect the way we live. The affluence which we call middle-class America will become a smaller and smaller island in a sea of poverty. By the year 1991 more than half of all the world's citizens were concentrated in eight developing countries: China, India, Indonesia, Brazil, Pakistan, Bangladesh, Nigeria and Mexico.[6] As recently as 1970, New York was the largest city on earth. By the end of the century, five may be larger, including three from developing nations: Mexico City (28 million), São Paulo, Brazil (25 million), and Bombay, India (15 million). Of the great cities of North America and Europe, only New York, Los Angeles and Moscow may even rank in the top twenty.[7] Within a decade, only five people in every one hundred will be North Americans.

This growing nonwhite, non-American world will be a world without:

without sufficient food to eat, without clean water to drink, without adequate shelter, without sanitation, without education, without the most basic necessities of life.

By the year 2010, Africa will be the fastest growing continent on earth, surging from its present 701 million to over one billion.[8] Yet in the 1980s total African food production actually decreased in the face of devastating drought which ravaged the center of the continent. It directly affected thirty-six countries, six severely in the region called the Sahel, a belt stretching west across the African midsection from Mauritania and Senegal in the west to Chad in the east.

Further east, famine has been severe in Ethiopia and Somalia. Fleeing this starvation, millions of refugees poured into their western neighbor, Sudan, compounding that country's already severe social and economic problems. A major famine hit the country, with more than four million Sudanese directly affected by starvation. Then-president of the Sudan, Gaafar Nimeiri, came to Washington to seek additional U.S. help. Before he could return, his nation was taken over by a military coup in the face of growing political and economic unrest.

In Somalia, widespread famine combined with anarchy led to massive starvation, beginning in the late 1980s. U.S. Marines stationed there began restoring order and ensuring food delivery by late 1992. Their work substantially reduced the threat of famine, but it did not restore order.

Some 900 million of the world's people live in dryland or desert regions. Though there is controversy over whether the agricultural problems of these regions are attributable to real desert expansion or to normal fluctuations in rainfall,[9] the problem has become serious enough to warrant a new global agreement, signed by more than 100 nations, to address desertification issues.[10]

Changing Times

Concern for the environment was more popular twenty years ago than now. The 1970s were rightly called the "decade of the environment," beginning in 1970 when Richard Nixon was signing into law the National Environmental Policy Act of 1969, or NEPA, as it came to be called. It was NEPA that gave birth to the Environmental Impact Statement, or EIS, that ponderous document that was to be required of every "major federal action" affecting the environment.

A surge of environmental legislation followed. The year 1970 alone saw the creation of the Environmental Protection Agency (EPA), the passage of the Environmental Quality Act, amendments to the Clean Air Act and the first "Earth Day," April 22. On that date, CBS news anchorman Walter Cronkite appeared, as usual, on the television screens of millions of Americans to present the *CBS Evening News.* Behind him in that telecast loomed a picture of the earth with a giant question mark and in bold letters the words "Can the world be saved?"[11]

Landmark environmental legislation continued to characterize the seventies, like the revised Endangered Species Act (1973), the Forest Reserves Management Act (1974, 1976) and the Surface Mining Control and Reclamation Act (1977), to name a few. But a clean environment soon proved to be more costly than the average American had bargained for. The expense and red tape of environmental regulation, coupled with economic downturn and even recession in traditionally strong segments of the American economy, led to rising resentment against the environmental movement. Resentment ran especially high in the American West, where growing anger over federal restrictions on the use of both public and private lands flared into open conflict in the so-called Sagebrush Rebellion.

Where the seventies had begun with NEPA, the eighties began with James Watt as secretary of the interior, freezes on land acquisition by the National Park Service, coal leases on public lands at bargain prices and a "wait-and-see" attitude toward the growing problem of acid rain. The decade ended with a grim reminder of the price of environmental carelessness. On March 24, 1989, the Exxon tanker *Valdez* ran aground in Alaskan coastal waters on the now infamous Bligh Reef. By April 10, oil from the *Valdez* had reached the shores of Alaska's Kenai Fjords National Park, and by May 2, Katmai National Park. Ecosystems whose integrity had been as uncompromised as any in the world had been radically and unpredictably altered.

Future Prospects

On April 22, 1990, twenty years after the first Earth Day, it was again celebrated. Highlighting changes made since 1970, major television networks scheduled documentaries and regular news features. Newspapers and national magazines allocated exceptional space for coverage of events. College and university campuses coordinated activities with local government offices. Publishers planned book publications to coincide with this global event.

In the years that have passed since the first Earth Day, environmentalists have expanded their ranks and taken up new environmental causes with renewed enthusiasm. And many ordinary, nonenvironmentalist Americans who only take out the trash also have made changes in lifestyle. In many communities landfill space is now at a premium and recycling is no longer an option but the law. In Illinois, grass clippings and yard waste can no longer be left with the garbage to go to the landfill. They must be composted on the owner's property or taken to a centrally located compost site. In addition to extending resources such as aluminum, glass and forests, the act of recycling takes on symbolic significance for the educational training of future generations. The throwaway generation of the seventies no longer has any place to throw away. Perhaps the effects will extend to the production of more durable products as environmental groups press for more control at the input end of the cycle rather than focusing on what to do with all the output items.

But more media coverage and greater popular awareness do not necessarily mean real changes or lasting solutions. We make a beginning when we move beyond "watching" environmental problems on the evening news to understanding the causes (and effects) of the problems we have so far only described. This understanding begins with a basic grasp of the cyclical nature of environmental systems.

Today, after many years of growth, many environmental organizations are facing declining memberships. The public is saturated with, and to some extent desensitized to, the magnitude of the environmental crisis. One can push the environmental compassion button only so many times before the response begins to fatigue. Yet the problems are no less real; in some cases now they are even worse.

Naming these problems individually would produce a long and intimidating list. But they can be understood in several broad categories. The most basic, and most serious, of our environmental problems are those which threaten basic systems of our planet's life support. The two most important of these are the potential for global warming (from the ever-expanding, human-caused increase in carbon dioxide emissions) and the depletion of stratospheric ozone (from the emission of chlorofluorocarbons, which is also human-induced).

Associated with these, and sometimes caused by them, are our planet's loss of natural habitats and the plant and animal species native to them. Local in their effects, these problems are nonetheless global in their scope. This category includes the well-documented problems of tropical deforestation and loss of biodiversity, as well as the sometimes not-so-well documented or well-known problems associated with losses of wetlands, temperate forests, tundra and alpine habitats, and others.

Finally, an entire category of different, but closely related, problems center on human consumption and pollution, and what to do with our own personal and industrial byproducts. In this category are the problems of acid precipitation ("acid rain"), solid and toxic waste disposal and various forms of air and water pollution. Exacerbating and underlying all of these problems is a continually growing human population, fast approaching six billion and not expected to level off until it reaches ten to fourteen billion individuals.

Before attempting to understand and address, in more detail, these problems, as well as their causes and effects, it is necessary to begin with a basic understanding of how matter and energy are processed in natural systems. It is in understanding how such systems *normally* work that we can better appreciate what results when they are disturbed and degraded.

Basic Ecological Cycles

Many of the most serious environmental problems facing our world today are symptomatic of disruptions or imbalances in the movements and transformations of matter within natural systems. To begin, we must describe the way our environment normally processes matter and energy when it is not polluted or stressed.

Think for a moment about the relation of such basic components as plants, animals, air, water and sunshine. Under normal conditions, the proportion of oxygen (20 percent) and carbon dioxide (0.03 percent) is regulated so that a dynamic balance is maintained. Green plants form carbohydrates and release oxygen in the presence of sunlight when water and carbon dioxide are available. The energy from the sun is also available in the water cycle; it evaporates moisture from the oceans and freshwater sources to form fog and clouds in the atmosphere. Temperature changes, with air currents, result in precipitation of water as rain, snow, sleet or hail, and so moisture is returned to the earth again. Unlike plants, animals release carbon dioxide and consume oxygen in their basic metabolic processes. To gain energy, they eat plants or other animals. To complete the cycle, some animal waste products contain nitrogen, phosphorus, calcium and other elements that are essential nutrients which plants absorb from the soil through their root systems. Death and decay of both plants and animals produce the ultimate ecologic economy. Their bodies release nutrients, helped by the activity of decomposer organisms, for new growth and life in a new generation of plants.

Much more detail could be provided about how each element cycles through individual environments, but that is not our purpose here. Rather, our aim is to show that humans too are part of this finely tuned system. In fact, they play an important role. As you might imagine, a balance of components is essential to keep things running smoothly. If you get too many animals in one place, too much energy from the sun without enough water, too much nitrogen and phosphorous in a shallow lake, or any of a multitude of other imbalances, the system becomes stressed, overloaded, and breaks down. A given area can only support a given population. The kind and quality of available resources limits the kind and quality of living things, including humans, that can be sustained on any area. Ecologists refer to this dynamic equilibrium between populations and their resources as *carrying capacity*. It is a concept that must become much more widely understood and applied in the careful management of planet Earth.

Critical Imbalances

The concept of carrying capacity is but one example of natural equilibria between populations and their resources. A concept even more foundational and essential to understanding the functioning of normal ecosystems is the Law of Conservation of Matter. Put simply, this law states that matter can neither be created nor destroyed, though it can be transformed physically and chemically. This means that the quantity of matter in the universe is constant.

The implications of this law are profound. There is no "away" where discarded matter can be thrown. Once introduced into a system, matter moves through that system, changed to different forms by physical and chemical processes, but it cannot simply disappear. In this way, nonliving material in the environment is maintained at relatively constant levels. In normal ecosystems the same matter may be used over and over again in different forms as it is involved in physical and chemical transformations. Equilibria also may be maintained through the processing of such matter by different kinds of living creatures.

Problems may arise when reactions and processes that maintain such equilibria are disrupted. From this standpoint, we can better understand the well-publicized problems of ozone.

Ozone can have both positive and negative effects on life and health. It depends on where the ozone is and how much there is of it. On a hot, humid summer day in the middle of rush-hour traffic in a large city there is usually a lot of ozone present that you could just as well do without. This ozone not only causes headaches and respiratory discomfort to humans but also damages plant growth and synthetic materials.

But in the upper atmosphere, ozone is beneficial to life on earth. It absorbs harmful ultraviolet light from the sun, preventing much of it from reaching the surface of the earth. But a hole has appeared in this ozone shield above Alaska, and a similar one exists above Antarctica in the southern hemisphere. In other nonpolar regions there are areas where the ozone layer has become dangerously thin. These reductions in ozone concentration are believed to be the result of human activity, especially the release of chlorofluorocarbons (CFCs) emitted from air conditioner coolants, aerosol sprays and the manufacture of Styrofoam.

This is not the atmosphere's only problem. Others also exist, created by similar kinds of critical imbalances and disruptions of natural equilibria. Increased levels of carbon dioxide in our air may contribute to global warming. This too is related to human activity, especially from the burning of fossil fuels. Atmospheric levels of carbon dioxide have increased by 25 percent since the onset of the Industrial Revolution in the nineteenth century.[12] A few degrees' increase in average global temperatures can have extreme consequences in agricultural production and in seawater levels throughout the world.

The growth of human populations in historic times has increased the destruction of many plant and animal habitats, as previously described. Many species are threatened, endangered or have become extinct due to human activity. The worldwide loss of tropical rainforests continues at a rapid rate. Because such rainforests are home to so many different kinds of plants and animals, this has led to a loss of species diversity worldwide. In the United States, freshwater marshes and wetlands also have been destroyed rapidly. Wetland destruction has been slowed by protection of federal law, but there is still a net loss of wetland acreage every year.

Human activity affects species diversity in every habitat, not just in these more dramatic examples. Whenever one kind of habitat is changed into another, equilibria between plant and animal populations and their resources are changed, and carrying capacities are affected.

Waste Much, Lose Much

It is not wetland drainage or tropical deforestation alone that leads to habitat and species loss. The reality of the Law of Conservation of Matter makes itself felt when habitats are destroyed simply to find places to put human waste. The problems associated with the dumping of garbage, household trash and toxic waste have reached critical levels. Many sanitary landfills will be filled to capacity in the next few years. Although an increasing trend to recycle may increase their life, the long-term solution must be a reduction of excess packaging and a public demand for more durable products. Both government and industry must combine forces and modify an existing economic system that is still insensitive to the problems of solid waste disposal.

In recent years we have learned that toxic wastes must be treated differently from other solid wastes. Paint thinners, crankcase oil, pesticides and other hazardous chemicals can cause damage to ground and surface water supplies if they are discarded with ordinary garbage. Over time, they leak downward through the soil to contaminate drinking water supplies, providing yet another vivid, and dangerous, illustration of the Law of Conservation of Matter. When this happens, there is not only a direct threat to human health but also the possibility of contaminating the living biological filter of secondary sewage treatment plants. So far the U.S. government's efforts to clean up toxic waste sites have been largely confined to identifying and listing over two thousand of them. Although the enabling legislation is in place, budget allocations do not begin to address the extensive cleanup costs involved, which may be in the billions of dollars.

One such site was in the Blackwell Forest Preserve in DuPage County, Illinois. In 1980 it was described as an environmental success story.[13] Originally called Mount Trashmore, it was cleaned up in a carefully designed process. A large hill was to be constructed of clay cubicles filled with garbage. The soil excavation sites produced from constructing these cubicles were to become recreational lakes for swimming, boating and fishing. For several years everything seemed to be going as planned. Then one day traces of hazardous chemicals (trihalomethanes) were found in one of the monitoring wells, and the swimming lake was closed. The site was suggested for the Environmental Protection Agency's notorious "Superfund" category, a list of the most badly and dangerously polluted sites in the country, and among the costliest to clean up. An investigation to determine the source of the dangerous chemicals at Mount Trashmore is still in progress as this book goes to press, but many think that the initial engineering design failed to provide any means of drainage for the rising head of groundwater created when the hill was constructed.

In energy conservation, the world continues to face a quietly growing crisis. Despite widespread acknowledgment that petroleum-based transportation and heating systems must be phased out during the twenty-first century, the United States still has no long-term energy policy. Extensive subsidies from the federal government to nuclear energy began after World War II in the "Atoms for Peace" programs. Both the development of nuclear energy as well as its promotion and regulation were under the authority of the Atomic Energy Commission. After many years and much agitation by environmentalists and the general public, the power of this agency was reduced by forming a Nuclear Regulatory Agency and separating it from the Department of Energy. Nuclear energy continues to be a controversial solution to the energy crisis. Not only does the problem of long-term disposal of nuclear waste remain unsolved, but the close connection between nuclear weapons and nuclear energy technology remains troublesome to many.

The responsibility to address these and other environmental problems is not only anchored in the motive of human survival, it is fundamentally rooted in the relationship of human beings to their Creator. "To obey is better than sacrifice" was the instruction given by the prophet Samuel to Israel's King Saul (1 Samuel 15:22). That is still the imperative today. On these issues, obedience will mean living within the carrying capacity of our environment in harmony with the cycles God has established within his creation. As we do so, the earth's environment will be enhanced, and future generations will be treated with the justice and equity they deserve.

Important as it is to describe and understand environmental problems, that is not the primary purpose of our book. The environmental crisis cannot be successfully treated merely as a series of scientific or technical problems. As biologist Garrett Hardin wrote so perceptively and prophetically in 1968, these are problems which have "no technical solution."[14] A comprehensive solution to these basic problems must address three critical questions:

☐ Who is God as Creator?

☐ What is the earth as his creation?

☐ Who are we as God's creatures in this creation?

Three Compelling Questions

At first it may seem liberating to view the world as an autonomous product of time, chance and change. This makes it a value-free environment governed only by competing self-interests. Yet humans, throughout history, have never been comfortable with that view. When confronted with the beauty of the physical world, we instinctively ascribe value to it. When faced with its grandeur, we are humbled. When shown its complexity, we seek comprehensive and rational explanation. Regardless of what we *say* about our philosophical positions, we *behave* as if we wanted and needed to find value in creation.

This behavior is rooted in the reality of God. God freely created a cosmos, including our earth, and in it reveals not only his work but also his personal characteristics. God called what he made good, thus making creation's value an integral part of its reality. We insult that value when we mistreat creation or its creatures, but our shame at this mistreatment reveals again that the value of creation is really there. If it were not, humans would not so despise themselves for destroying rainforests, exterminating species, making holes in the ozone or polluting the ocean. So the reality of God and his good creation hem us in. Whenever we try to address the value of creation we find that we must first address God.

Yet even Christians may miss the mark here. No one is so far from God as a Pharisee, one who attempts to control and manipulate an image of God built by confining him solely to propositional statements, even biblical propositional statements. No one can be so far from God as one who would separate God's *word* from God's *work*. This view of God is nowhere shattered more brutally than in the first chapter of Genesis: "God *said* . . . and it *was* . . ." It is only in seeing and understanding the *work* of God in and through creation that we will fully understand the *word* of God in Scripture. In Scripture alone, the activity of God can be difficult to comprehend. But to those who also study his creation, his work is both comprehensible and alive.

What, then, is this earth? It is, foundationally, both a work of God and a revelation of God. The earth itself and all its creatures have been created by God, exist for the pleasure and purpose of God, and derive both their reality and their value from God. They are sustained by God even in the midst of death and decay, and one day will be revealed, with humans, as objects of God's redemptive purpose.

Who, then, are we as human beings? Though made in God's image, we are selfish, like all creatures, and instinctively look to our own needs first. Yet unlike other creatures, we feel shame at our own selfishness, and we inexplicably feel at once a sense of both authority and responsibility toward our surroundings. We cut down trees. We return and plant new ones. We say, in the present age, that we want to be "one with nature." Then we rush out to save, manage and restore nature, for its own good, by our activity. We are not content with *biology*. We feel compelled to develop *conservation biology* and insist on applying our knowledge and skills to benefit other creatures. We cannot rest with simply studying *ecology*. We are driven to devise *restoration ecology*, restoring habitats we have blighted, even at great expense to ourselves.

At every turn we feel driven to recognize value in creation and then to protect and preserve the value that we find. But all of this is strange, or even cruelly perplexing, *only if there is no God.* And so the Bible tells us that is what the fool has said in his heart (Psalm 14:1). But those who say "God *is*" find that life's problems, though vexing, can be understood. Those who know God as Creator know that his creation can be enjoyed, valued and celebrated without doubt or guilt. For those who know themselves as both *creatures,* made from dust, and *stewards,* tilling, keeping and naming in God's image, there is purpose, power and dignity in being human. There is conscious joy and value in caring for creation. And for those who know both, there are whole worlds of life with God that can never be known to those who confine God to words only.

Our book is not only, or even primarily, about environmental problems. It is about God's view and value of this place, this earth. And it is about our place in this earth before God. Will you read further? We invite you, as Philip invited Nathanael, "Come and see."

Questions for Thought and Discussion

1. Several global environmental problems were mentioned in this chapter. Which ones seem most important to you at this moment? Why?

2. Have you seen a California condor or a whooping crane lately? How important are endangered species to you? How important are they to God?

3. Is there a pressing environmental issue in your local area? To what extent have you been involved in it? To what extent should you be more involved?

4. Is it appropriate to raise the environmental issues of this chapter in a church setting? What principles or teachings of Scripture have relevance to these issues?

2
God the Creator

*The beginning of the Christian view of nature
is the concept of creation: that God was there
before the beginning and God created
everything out of nothing. From this, we
understand that creation is not an extension of
the essence of God. Created things have an
existence in themselves. They are really there.*
FRANCIS SCHAEFFER [1]

N O IDEA IN HUMAN HISTORY HAS HAD MORE IMPACT THAN THE
first five words of Scripture, "In the beginning God created."
It is an idea so radical that it finds no parallel in ancient myth
or modern philosophy. No culture was without its story of creation, but
none could conceive of creation ex nihilo, out of nothing. To an
ancient people surrounded by pagan cultures, God revealed his true
nature, even as he reveals it today to a modern people steeped in
twentieth-century secularism.

Ancient Views of God and Creation
The dominant creation myth of the ancient Near East was the Enuma
Elish, one of several Babylonian creation stories. In its polytheistic view
of many gods in a chaotic universe, Marduk, the hero god, slays the
monster goddess Tiamat and the servant monsters she has created. The
earth is formed from Tiamat's dismembered body. Humankind is
fashioned from the body of a god, Kingu, who is sacrificed for his part
in helping Tiamat. There is no dignity for humanity in this creation.
"Blood I will mass and cause bones to be," says Marduk. "I will establish
a savage, 'man' shall be his name. He shall be charged with the service
of the gods that they might be at ease."[2] But Marduk himself is no real

creator, only a craftsman making a tool for his own use. The cosmos itself, in Enuma Elish, existed before the gods, and they are but products of it.

Other pagan myths offer an equally pessimistic view of humanity's place and destiny in the universe. One example of an influential view in ancient cultures is the Mesopotamian story of Atrahasis. This story begins with the gods already established in an organized society. The greater (management) gods have assigned the more numerous lesser (labor) gods the heavy work of digging canals on the earth. After years of long and oppressive conditions, they protest, form a picket line at the foreman's (the god Enlil's) house and set their tools on fire.

An emergency management council is called, and the craft god, Ea, has a plan. The birth goddess, Mami, is assigned to create humans, and they will take over the canal work. One of the gods is sacrificed to provide the capital. Mami shapes the mixture into fourteen humans (seven male and seven female) and puts them in a place called "the house of destiny" for ten months. At the end of their gestation they are born into the world.[3]

The worldview of today's culture is deeply indebted to Greek philosophy and to the Greek mythology out of which it arose. Though these arose later than the writings of Enuma Elish and Atrahasis, which were contemporaries of the Genesis account, the Greek view is worth looking at in detail. Today the increasing interest in the Greek worldview is based on the assumption that it offers a coherent picture of the cosmos and of humanity's place in it. It does not.

Several of the key elements in Enuma Elish are shared in Greek mythology and later incorporated into Greek philosophy. A plurality of gods is produced from an existing cosmos. Eventually there is civil war, and one god, Zeus, emerges victorious, killing or banishing his enemies and rewarding his allies.

But unlike other mythologies, Greek mythology makes no attempt to account for the human race: it is taken as a given. Humans are no object of love for Zeus. Rather, in his anger at the titan Prometheus, who gave them fire, Zeus directs his vengeance at Prometheus and humans. To torment men he creates a fair maiden, Pandora, and makes her, in the word of the Greek writer Hesiod, a "spine-chilling, untouchable booby trap,"[4] because she is given a gift of pain and sorrow for men from every Olympian god. These are contained in a jar (not a box, as the common expression would imply), along with the gift of hope, and Pandora, after being sent to earth, opens the lid. All manner of evil flies forth to afflict men randomly. Pandora slaps down the lid when she realizes what is happening, but it is too late. Only hope is trapped inside. So Zeus's malice against humans triumphs. "Full is the earth," wrote Hesiod, "full is the sea of evil. During the day, afflictions come to mortals; and at night they go to and fro wherever they will, inflicting evils. . . . Thus, there is no way to escape Zeus's plan."[5] Out of these elements Greek philosophy would later identify God with nature, see his activity as initial and theoretical, but not continuing or made by free choice, and view him as a craftsman of natural forms but not a true creator.[6]

Despite their differences, the Babylonian, Mesopotamian and Greek explanations of creation and of humanity's place in it have much in common with each other, but crucial differences with the Genesis account. The former see the universe and its material existence as the preexisting foundation from which all things, even the divine, arise. Genesis says God is preexistent, and it is from him that all things arise. The ancient myths see human beings demeaned by the gods and driven to do their will by force, or else tortured and punished by the gods for human presumptions and personal initiatives. Genesis makes human beings creatures created in the image of God, and their service to him an expression of both their freedom and their humanity. The pagan myths make the world and its creatures accidents created by chance and soon at odds with the gods who inhabit the universe with them. Genesis, by the word of God, calls the creation "good" and blesses it to be fruitful and multiply. So the startling ideas of Genesis confronted their pagan contemporaries as radically as they confront the world today.

The Radical Revelation

It was to a culture steeped in these ideas that a living God spoke, revealing the true nature of himself and what he had made, of the place of humankind, of the nature of good and evil, and of human hope and destiny.

"In the beginning God created the heavens and the earth." With unequaled dignity and beauty, the writer of Genesis reveals a wealth of knowledge about God in a single sentence. First, *God is preexistent.* He does not emanate from a preexistent, eternal cosmos. He is the one entity that is eternal and preexistent. Second, *God is transcendent.* He is not the same as what he has made, and he does not add to or subtract from himself to make it.

Third, *God is a creator,* and that means he is free. A craftsman god can work only according to a predetermined plan and purpose in constructing a tool for a particular use. That tool can only be one thing, not another. Nature, as the work of a craftsman, was not free, but predetermined. Therefore, its reality was best understood by deductive reasoning, not by extensive observation. But Greek science ultimately failed because nature is not like Euclidean geometry, nor is God like Euclid. God's creation, though reasonable, is unique. It could have been something other than what it is, but God gave form from a void, and a uniqueness out of a myriad of possibilities, to a heaven and an earth which had neither.

Finally, *the universe itself is a creation.* As Francis Schaeffer said, "It is really there."[7] It is not an illusion. Its material substance is neither an imperfection, as Aristotle thought, a necessary evil, as Plato thought, nor an illusion, as Buddha thought. Rather, as soon as nature is understood to be a *creation,* we understand that its material substance is not some imperfection in its form, but the essence of it. That is why we can now begin to deal honestly with the things in creation as *creatures,* not as imperfect, evil or unreal. And we can begin to see ourselves not as souls trapped in physical bodies (which even some Christians mistakenly believe) but as creatures with a composite and integrated nature: body, mind and spirit.

The consequences of these truths must not be allowed to escape us. A current perception in Western Christendom—that what is material is evil and what is nonmaterial is spiritual—is not a biblical view but a Greek one. As long as it persists, it will prevent Christians from fully knowing God as Creator and from experiencing the value and joy of his good creation.

God the Originator

So God as Creator is no less than the "prime mover," but he is also much, much more. God is not an impersonal force setting a universe in motion like the cue ball on a billiards table, but an artist-creator designing a great work. But he is not like a wall painter whose wall is still a wall even after it is painted. God is an artist who creates a picture from nothing but his own creativity. God makes the universe his creation. God chooses. And like God, the creation exhibits his choices, as well as the ability to make some of its own.

The instrument of creation is the Word of God (John 1:1, 14). As Dietrich Bonhoeffer said, "Creation is not an 'effect' of the Creator whence we would derive a necessary connection with the cause (Creator). It is a work created in the freedom of the Word. . . . The essential point is not that the word has effects but that God's word is itself work. That which in us breaks hopelessly asunder is for God indissolubly one."[8] With God, word and work are one, and the creation powerfully reveals this essential element of God's character.

"And God saw that it was good." There is no place in the Christian mind for the view that created things are evil any more than that they are divine. They are creatures, but they are good. They are good not in themselves, but because their Creator, who is good, acknowledges them, calls them his own and pronounces them good. And that is the right and proper kind of goodness for created things to have.

And so the ancient Israelites were plunged into a totally different view of themselves, their God and his creation from anything they could have absorbed from their neighbors. Instead of many gods, one. Instead of a transcendent cosmos, a transcendent God. Instead of an artificer, a Creator. Instead of evil matter, good creatures. And instead of hopeless slaves, free humans in the image of God.

Humanity as God's Creation

"Let us make man in our image, in our likeness, and let them rule over the fish of the sea and the birds of the air, over the livestock, over all the earth, and over all the creatures that move along the ground" (Genesis 1:26). The rule of the earth is not given to underling gods, as in the pagan stories of creation, but to humans; humans share God's work and witness on the earth. We are not slaves created to dig canals, but "the mirror of God" in Bonhoeffer's words, according to his likeness. And we are not the objects of God's malice and anger, but the honored subjects of his care.

Yet while the biblical view exalts humans as pagan superstitions do not, it also humbles humans in a way they do not. In ancient mythology, humans are formed from the bones and blood of a god. They share the essence of the divine. Humans are, in that view, completely different from other creatures. But in Genesis, humans are creatures themselves. Though sharing God's likeness (by God's choice, not ours), we do not share God's essence. Humans are not divine. It was the unanimous verdict of ancient religions that man, or at least a part of him, was divine. But that claim is pointedly rejected and violently shattered by the Christian doctrine of creation.[9]

Far from being divine, humans brought evil to a good creation. But God, unlike Zeus, was not the author of that evil, nor did he slam down the jar's lid, trapping hope inside.

God the Sustainer

The story of Genesis is the story of creation and Creator. But the Bible knows of no Creator who is not also Sustainer and Provider. "Now the LORD God had planted a garden in the east, in Eden. . . . And the LORD God made all kinds of trees to grow out of the ground—trees that were pleasing to the eye and good for food" (Genesis 2:8-9). There is no hint of the deistic, Enlightenment concept of God as the great watchmaker who winds up the universe and then leaves it to take a licking and keep on ticking. While the universe is, on most days, a regular and orderly place in which God works through regular patterns, which science refers to as natural laws, God is not dependent on them, nor do they exist independent of him. For this reason the Bible speaks of God "sustaining all things by his powerful word" (Hebrews 1:3). And were he to withdraw that power, even for an instant, all that is would collapse into nothingness, as though it had never been.

But the provision of God is not an impersonal provision, a cosmic food-stamp distribution. It is spoken of in Scripture as a direct, personal and caring provision for all creatures. "He makes springs pour water into the ravines; it flows between the mountains. They give water to all the beasts of the field; the wild donkeys quench their thirst. . . . He waters the mountains from his upper chambers; the earth is satisfied by the fruit of his work" (Psalm 104:10-11, 13). His provision is the source of life, his withdrawal of it the source of death.

> These all look to you
>> to give them their food at the proper time.
> When you give it to them,
>> they gather it up;
> when you open your hand,
>> they are satisfied with good things.
> When you hide your face,
>> they are terrified;
> when you take away their breath,
>> they die and return to the dust.
> When you send your Spirit,
>> they are created,
>> and you renew the face of the earth. (Psalm 104:27-30)

As his provision is not limited to humans, neither does it exclude them. So the Scripture is not embarrassed to speak of many of the "blessings of God" not in spiritual terms only, as qualities of mind and heart, but of material substance as well, as God's good gifts of creation.

> About Joseph he said:
> "May the LORD bless his land
>> with the precious dew from heaven above
>> and with deep waters that lie below;
> with the best the sun brings forth
>> and the finest the moon can yield;
> with the choicest gifts of the ancient mountains,
>> and the fruitfulness of the everlasting hills;
> with the best gifts of the earth and its fullness
>> and the favor of him who dwelt in the burning bush."
>> (Deuteronomy 33:13-16)

God the Redeemer

God is not only One who makes and then sustains but also One who will one day redeem and perfect. His plan for creation is redemption from the evil that has entered it. The first action of God toward this world (that of creating) is of the past and the second (sustaining) of the present, but this last act of creation (redeeming) is of the future. And out of its promise comes the hope of the world.

For the creation was subjected to frustration, not by its own choice,
but by the will of the one who subjected it, in hope that the creation
itself will be liberated from its bondage to decay and brought into
the glorious freedom of the children of God. (Romans 8:20-21)

Yet this redemption is also a present and ongoing work. Christ's death
began the redemptive process that will be fully realized in the future.
His death will change not merely you and me but also the entire cosmos
in which we live.

The Celebration of Creation

Out of this context, the Hebrews did not respond by trying to prove
the existence of God from creation, but rather assumed and acknowledged God's work in creation and then rejoiced in it.[10] "The heavens
declare the glory of God; the skies proclaim the work of his hands"
(Psalm 19:1). What stands out most in the Hebrew view of nature was
the ability to see a created thing and *rejoice* without shame or restraint
in its beauty and mystery. "There are three things that are too amazing
for me," wrote Solomon, "four that I do not understand: the way of an
eagle in the sky, the way of a snake on a rock, the way of a ship on the
high seas, and the way of a man with a maiden" (Proverbs 30:18-19).

The fruit that grows from any philosophy which makes nature the
result of time plus the impersonal plus chance is the loss of joy. But the
joy of nature, or more correctly, *creation*, is the joy of the Creator over
his creation which he imparts to us. Said God to Job: "Look at the
behemoth[11] which I made along with you and which feeds on grass like
an ox. What strength he has in his loins, what power in the muscles of
his belly! . . . He ranks first among the works of God" (Job 40:15-16,
19). What joy indeed! And not because it is useful (for behemoth is not
humanly useful), but because it is wondrous. Indeed, wondrous even
in destruction and in frightening power.

And what could be more powerful, more wondrous, than the great
Creator himself—symbolized by the reflections of the psalmist on
God's presence in the thunderstorm.

The voice of the LORD is powerful;
   the voice of the LORD is majestic.
The voice of the LORD breaks the cedars;
   the LORD breaks in pieces the cedars of Lebanon. . . .

The LORD shakes the Desert of Kadesh.
The voice of the LORD twists the oaks
    and strips the forest bare.
And in his temple all cry, "Glory!" (Psalm 29:4-5, 8-9)

And rising above fear, the one who knows both the Creator and his creation answers "Glory!" as well. Eagle and snake and storm and monster—joy comes in power when we truly see the cosmos as the creation of God, and when we truly come to understand what it means to call God "Creator." Then we can understand these words of James Nash: "God is the Pantocrator, the sole governor and final benefactor, the sovereign source of all being and becoming, the ultimate provider and universal proprietor, the originator and systematic organizer."[12]

A Renewed Worship

When I was a college professor in Indiana, I used to take annual autumn trips with small groups of students to northern Michigan. Our days were filled with living examples of the textbook's concepts: succession on sand dunes, the flow of groundwater into marshes, the formation of soil in a forest. Our time in the college van and in the evenings was filled with study and reflection on the Word of God related to the creation we were seeing.

Many students told me this experience was a highlight of their time in the biology course. I was not surprised. What was surprising was that many more told me it was the most powerful spiritual experience they had during their time at college. Now this was an amazing thing, seeing that this was a Christian college focusing on vocational preparation of young men and women for full-time ministry. Every course was devoted to the presentation of the Word of God, at both personal and scholastic levels. Christian service work and church attendance were required. Chapel was held daily, and entire days were set aside for what was called "spiritual emphasis," featuring the best speakers the regional and national Christian community could provide. Why then should students speak of a biology field trip as their most memorable "spiritual" experience, when the instructor's primary goal was for scientific education?

The answer points to a deficiency in modern worship and spiritual life, particularly in Christian education. We have so personalized the

Christian experience, we have so described commitment to Christ as a state of mental introspection, we have so defined faith as a quality of the intellect, that we have created one-dimensional Christians. They are truly sincere and devoted, but their teachers and pastors push their devotion ever inward, never outward. The result is a life that often grows bleary and bleak, and every attempt to experience the glory of God is an ever deeper plunge within the heart and head. But the Hebrew mind understood that the great power of God is displayed in his *works,* and in the beauty, enjoyment and understanding of them. It is wind and rain in the face on a treeless hill, the mud of a marsh beneath one's feet, and the sound of whirring wings at sunset that give examples of what joy and beauty *are.* Without these examples from the living laboratory of creation, the lectures of Scripture fall on deaf ears.

Modern worship must return to an emphasis on the joy of the works and wonders of God in order that joy may become once again an experience instead of a concept. Joy must be a taste, a touch and a smell, not an idea only, and God must be not only the Lord of heaven above but also the Maker of earth beneath. Until these practices find their place in right worship of God, it is not to be wondered at that our devotions are insipid, our prayers bland and our state of mind a million miles from the "joy unspeakable" described in Scripture as the proper state of Christians.

Our hope to attain this cannot come from worship only, but from our thought, teaching and practice of science. And if the church has often failed us in the first case, Christian educational institutions have even more often failed us in the second.

A Repentant Science

There are elements in science which a Christian can practice with joy and honor. God created a real and good world, so there is legitimate basis for empirical research and joy in discovery. God is rational, so the universe can be understood by reason. But God is also free, so the universe cannot be understood by reason alone, but reason coupled with investigation and guided by inspiration. And because we are created in God's image, we are rational as God is rational, and our insights are real insights about real things that can lead to real truth.

But science, as it is actually practiced today, has taken away many of these elements and added others. It has taken away much of the joy that ought to characterize science, and added much that is only human ego. It has taken away the concept of humility in science as rightful service toward a Creator, and added pride in science as a means by which humans depose their Creator and make themselves the master and measure of all creation.

The modern college education, particularly in the sciences, is often a fragmented and disconnected intellectual desert. This creates individuals who are themselves disconnected. They are professionals separated from their own persons. In this state of progressive mental disintegration, no one, Christian or non-Christian, can rediscover their own place and their own center—both of which are God's prerequisites for acceptable worship. If the Christian community is to rediscover right worship and service to God as Creator, and demonstrate that to others, then the Christian college must begin to teach not a "better" science which apes and competes with the state universities, but a different science. It must teach a repentant science that does not pull, tear and destroy the fabric of creation simply on the hopeful chance of making one interesting discovery. We must begin to teach students how to celebrate creation and not merely measure it. And we must make these things the foundations of our teaching, not merely a "devotional" appendage. And the parents who commit their children to the care of these teachers and their institutions must insist on these changes, and not merely accept the way things are.

There is a difference between a person who is a steward and a person who simply has an agenda for stewardship. "So then, men ought to regard us," Paul wrote to the church at Corinth, "as servants of Christ and as those entrusted with [stewards of] the secret things of God. Now it is required that those who have been given a trust must prove faithful" (1 Corinthians 4:1-2). And Jesus said of stewards, "Who then is the faithful and wise manager, whom the master puts in charge of his servants to give them their food allowance at the proper time? It will be good for that servant whom the master finds doing so when he returns. I tell you the truth, he will put him in charge of all his possessions" (Luke 12:42-44). The church of Christ does not need another "ism," like Christian environmentalism, to grow strong in faith. It does need to know God as Creator. It does not need to become another agency for stewardship. It does need to learn how to become a community of stewards.

It is these things that a repentant science could bring to us, not only new agendas but new people. And not merely new subjects for intellectual and abstract study, but new knowledge of a living God. And it is both appropriate and timely that the Christian college should begin to address and teach science in this manner. For the Bible never considers a truth to be known until it controls the life of the one who hears it. So the Christian community in general, and the Christian college in particular, must begin to chart the course for a science controlled by a knowledge of God the Creator, and the celebration of his glorious works.

A Synthesis: Why Do We Call It Creation?

It is significant that the Hebrews never referred to the world around them as "nature." They spoke of "creation," or the created order. We understand the distinction when we consider carefully what we mean by the word *nature* and by the words we derive from it, like *natural* or *naturally*. When we use the latter two in a sentence, we mean something that happens on its own, by itself, without design or interference. For example, "When the farmer did not plow his field, the weeds came up *naturally*." Or, "I know what I did was wrong, but it felt so *natural*." Perhaps an example closer to our point would be "The park seemed more *natural* because no people lived in it." In every case, we use these terms to describe events that happen because of the properties of the system. When we speak of the world as "nature," we speak of it as a self-generating, self-sustaining system, and we mentally (even if unconsciously) exclude ourselves from it. We consider ourselves a "nonnormal" part of the world. This leads us to conclude that the best we can do for nature is to remove ourselves from it. Nature is "too good for us."

Many people who have never consciously examined the merits of this type of thinking still live their lives and, in some cases, their careers, as if this were true. We see by their actions, their persistent efforts to remove themselves and all sign of human impact from designated "natural" areas, and by their shame (there is no other word for it) in being human, that this idea controls their response and reaction to the external world. It may be an idea that never had the courtesy to actually knock for entrance, introduce itself or express its true intentions, but now it is nonetheless the landlord of their thoughts.

Whatever else might be said of this idea, it is not a biblical one. The Hebrews called the world around them a *creation* because (1) they believed that it was unable to exist by itself and so must be sustained by a *Creator,* and (2) they saw themselves as *creatures,* things made and existing with other creatures in the world, all for the purposes and pleasures of God.

We would do well to cultivate and create this kind of thinking again. We can begin by being more careful of how we speak of the world, consciously rejecting the word *nature* and deliberately using the word *creation.* This simple change of speech would make a great difference in us. To call the world *creation* acknowledges that it (1) is made by God, (2) exists for the pleasure of God, (3) is sustained by God and (4) includes humans.

To speak in this way also reminds us of some essential denials: (1) the world did not create itself; (2) the world does not exist for its own purposes and pleasures (nor do we); (3) the world does not sustain itself; and (4) we as humans are not separate from it but part of it. What a difference one little word can make.

Questions for Thought and Discussion

1. What are the characteristics of God's witness in creation? What does that tell you about God?

2. What is God to creation other than its Creator? In Psalm 104, what is the psalmist's source of joy in creation?

3. How would you determine whether a person thought that the world around her or him was nature or creation? How would you demonstrate through personal actions and traits this distinction in yourself?

4. Why is a right understanding of these ideas important in the way we live today?

3
The Value of Creation

There is no speech or language
where their voice is not heard.
Their voice goes out into all the earth,
their words to the ends of the world.
P S A L M   1 9 : 3 - 4

THE WORDS OF DAVID IN PSALM 19 REPRESENT A REMARKABLE IN-
tegration as well as a profound juxtaposition. In these few words,
David beautifully describes God's two great "books": the book
of God's word, revealed in Scripture, and the book of God's work,
revealed in creation—what theologians would call *special revelation* and
general revelation, respectively. But David has done more than describe
them. He has dramatically stated the awesome possibility of knowing
God through each.

In the works of creation, God's revelation is always and everywhere
available to be seen and understood by men (Romans 1:18-22). Yet
though the witness is pervasive ("Their voice goes out into all the earth,
their words to the ends of the world"), it is inarticulate.[1] Well did C. S.
Lewis call nature "this dumb witch." As Dietrich Bonhoeffer noted,
God's works do not bear witness of God themselves, but bear witness
to God because his Word bears witness to them. God acknowledges that
they are his works and so claims their witness to him from his own
Word.[2]

So it is that general revelation, by itself, can teach precisely nothing
of God. Yet its revelation is not without value, for creation can provide
powerful illustrations of what Scripture teaches only as concept. If you

want to understand the concept of "glory" you must study your Bible. But once you have learned the concept, creation can give you a picture, vivid, splendid and real, of what glory might be like, though at best only a shadow of the heavenly substance.[3]

So creation cannot make revelations about Scripture, but the consistent revelation that Scripture makes about creation is that it is "good" (Genesis 1). As Bonhoeffer said, "Again and again we read, 'And God saw that it was good.' This signifies two things for us. God's work is good as the unimpaired form of the will of God. But it is good only in the way that the creaturely can be good, because the Creator views it, acknowledges it as his own and says of it, 'It is good.' "[4] This is the fundamental point of God's Word about God's work. But today the failure to grasp and the refusal to acknowledge this foundational promise about creation is at the heart of a significant crisis of value in conservation ethics. As Hosea wrote centuries before of those who abandon the ethics of God to construct their own, "They sow the wind and reap the whirlwind" (Hosea 8:7).

The Tucson Paradox
Tucson, Arizona, is one of the fastest-growing cities in America. John Naisbitt identifies it in his book *Megatrends* as one of the "ten great cities of opportunity."[5] The city is watered by a great underground aquifer, slowly stored through the ages by the seepage of surface runoff collected hundreds of meters beneath the ground. This aquifer was being depleted at the rate of 84 billion gallons a year.[6] Such a rapid depletion threatened the city's growth, especially its industrial growth, by adversely affecting its water bond rating. So Tucson acted. Through a massive public education campaign, Tucson cut per capita water consumption by 25 percent in only two years.[7] Yet every day Tucson's population experiences a net gain of three hundred new people.[8] So the depletion not only continues, it worsens. City leaders expect Tucson's population to double in forty-eight years.[9] If their predictions are accurate, the aquifer will be dry in fifty.[10]

This is the tragedy of the "Tucson Paradox."[11] Everyone is conserving, and nothing is being saved. Many have called for humanity to find a new ethic and throw away the old. Where have these new ethics led us?

By itself, the practice of conservation does not guarantee the preservation of any natural resource, for conservation's thrift can be made the slave of materialism's greed. In Tucson, the ultimate goal is growth, for growth means income. Water conservation was not a goal but only a means to that end. Water was not saved for water's sake, but for growth's sake. But no one can serve God and mammon.

Modern humans, deprived of even a mirror of the image of God, make themselves the measure of all things. They recognize that they live in a physical environment, and that from that environment they draw life. They recognize that they must conserve to ensure a continued supply of vital resources. They try to preserve favorable aspects of the environment because they enjoy their beauty, or because they enjoy the creatures which live there. But of everything, they are the center. It is unquestioned that the modern way of life must go on, with all the natural resources that sustain it. What they do not value, they will not sustain. The question of their own selfishness is never even addressed.

Wendell Berry described this predicament well in an essay entitled "Two Economies":

One of the favorite words of the industrial economy is "control." We want to keep things "under control.". . . But we are always setting out to control something we refuse to limit, and so we make control a permanent and a doomed enterprise. If we will not limit causes there can be no controlling of effects. What is to be the fate of self-control in an economy that encourages unlimited selfishness?[12]

Nicholas Wolterstorff echoes Berry's sentiments. In *Until Justice and Peace Embrace* he wrote, "The economic sphere has come to dominate all others: our society has become economized. . . . Like a cancerous growth, the economy has violated 'the sovereignty of the spheres.' "[13] And it has. In our divided world the economy is pitted against the environment, and the care of creation against gainful employment.

In the United States the example that has captured our attention is the controversy over the endangered spotted owl in the old-growth forests of the Pacific Northwest. The news media simplify the problem to a choice between saving the owl and maintaining the timber industry, and so distort real issues. The reality is far different. The actual question at stake is whether forests of the Pacific Northwest and elsewhere are truly being managed on a sustained-yield basis. Much independent opinion and study has concluded that they are not. The U.S. Forest Service, the federal agency that has primary responsibility for the management of our national forests, has come under increasing criticism for its economic practices and policies of selling timber. Oregon's Department of Employment reported that from 1977 to 1987 the state lost over twelve thousand jobs in logging and wood processing, a 15 percent decline. That decline occurred during a period in which wood taken from national forests increased by 10 percent.[14] Tim Hermach, president of the National Forest Council, concluded that the drop in employment occurred during periods of increased timber harvesting because 60 percent of all Pacific Northwest timber was exported unfinished. Writing in *The New York Times* in September 1991, Hermach declared, "Like a third world colony, we have turned what's left of our national resources into a source of raw materials for others."[15]

User Satisfaction

Some believe that the answer is preservation, to lock the best of creation away and allow only nonconsumptive uses (hiking, backpacking, camping, birdwatching and the like). Surely this would save what is valuable and beautiful. But would it? Professionals in outdoor recreation management have long been guided by a principle called "user satisfaction." This simply means that a quality outdoor recreational experience is determined by how well it lives up to the human participant's "satisfaction level"—that is, the individual's expectations. The old saying that "beauty is in the eye of the beholder" can now be quantified and analyzed. For outdoor recreation, it should then be easy to identify which areas should be preserved. They should be the areas that provide the highest levels of user satisfaction.[16] One would think that if this criterion is used, natural areas which humans "like" would surely be saved.

If only it were really so. Recent studies in outdoor recreation have identified a disturbing trend. Over time, people show an amazing adaptability to adjust to a lower and lower quality of outdoor recreation opportunity *without loss of satisfaction*. A number of river recreation studies, for example, have indicated that increasingly crowded conditions have had little or no effect on participant satisfaction levels.[17] But this finding is not limited to river recreation. Daniel Dustin and Leo McAvoy report that

> people appear to be growing less sensitive to the environmental degradation that inevitably accompanies crowding. In a study of boaters and campers visiting the Apostle Island National Lakeshore in northern Wisconsin . . . investigators found that as use levels increase, recent visitors became more tolerant of environmental degradation.[18]

The implications of these findings should disturb us. Recreation planning and management based on user satisfaction can actually perpetuate and contribute to the decline of the environment itself.[19] How could the great conservationist Aldo Leopold have known how closely he struck the mark when years ago he wrote, "Perhaps our grandsons, having never seen a wild river, will never miss the chance to set a canoe in singing waters"?[20] That telling statement is as tragic as it is true. The human species, precisely because it is so adaptable, stands in danger of losing forever the ability to perceive creation's beauty. Yes, humankind is adaptable. So adaptable, in fact, that we can adapt to hell on earth and never know we are its prisoners. René Dubos described our condition well:

> Life in the modern city has become a symbol of the fact that man can become adapted to starless skies, treeless avenues, shapeless buildings, tasteless bread, joyless celebrations, spiritless pleasures— to a life without reverence for the past, love for the present, or hope for the future.[21]

There is more to life than survival. There is more to creation than preservation. If human values and pleasures are the only goal of creation's protection, then those values and pleasures will be preserved while creation is destroyed.

Dead Ends and New Roads

The world has identified the Judeo-Christian ethic toward creation as the environmental villain and thrown it aside. In its place it has constructed ethics of its own making. But these are ethics of confusion, ethics of "no answer." "My people have committed two sins," said the Lord to Jeremiah. "They have forsaken me, the spring of living water, and have dug their own cisterns, broken cisterns that cannot hold water" (Jeremiah 2:13).

The great failure of modern environmental ethics has been its failure to establish the value of creation. The value of creation cannot be set by human money or human use. Neither, at the other extreme, can it be established by a pantheistic exaltation of nature which reduces humans to only animals. The ultimate value of creation can never be found within the creation itself. Out of these "no answer" ethics our problems, and our sorrows, have been spawned. As author Wendell Berry stated,

> The mentality of conservation is divided, and disaster is implicit in its division. It is divided between its intentional protection of some aspects of "the environment" and its inadvertent destruction of others. It is variously either vacation-oriented or crisis-oriented. For the most part, it is not yet sensitive to the impact of daily living upon the sources of daily life.[22]

There is an answer, and there is a value—a value of creation independent of anything that humans may do to creation or for creation. But for that answer, and that value, we must take a different road.

A Question of Value

Extensive knowledge and thrilling experience are not sufficient to produce a genuine ethic. The question of value is at the heart of it, and all ethics stand or fall on their ability to define value, to tell us what is the supreme good. The ultimate conservationist, Aldo Leopold, understood this well. He wrote:

> It is inconceivable to me that an ethical relation to the land can exist without love, respect, and admiration for land, and a high regard for its value. By value, I, of course, mean something far broader than economic value; I mean value in the philosophical sense.[23]

And only a clear understanding of value can lead to right and decisive action. Dietrich Bonhoeffer expressed it well in poetry.

> Do and dare what is right, not swayed by the whim of the moment.
> Bravely take hold of the real, not dallying now with what might be.
> Not in the flight of ideas but only in action is freedom.
> Make up your mind and come out into the tempest of the living.[24]

What a sad commentary on our times that many officials charged to do what is right with regard to the environment act with a timidity and hesitancy a million miles from the passion for right action that Bonhoeffer described. But perhaps the blame is not wholly theirs. Perhaps they lack passion because no true value has ever really captured their hearts.

Anyone who has real and recurring contact with God's creation senses the value and beauty within it. But it can be difficult to understand these feelings, much less express them. What is this story written in our bones, which leaps to life at the sight of God's creatures? "A thing too amazing for me," wrote Solomon, "the way of an eagle in the sky." Who wrote the story there? Who cast this shadow on our minds? Who sang the song we cannot remember, yet long to hear again? What image of the past betrays us?

The Good Creation

"In the beginning God created the heavens and the earth." Formless and void, a cosmos is formed out of chaos, spoken into existence by a transcendent God, a God truly independent and above nature, not an evolutionary product of it. The world and universe flow from the expression of his thought. Order, light and harmony come from chaos, darkness and discord. No human spectator surveys the scene. God alone, in company with angels, witnesses the creation.

> God said, "Let there be light," and there was light. God saw that the light was good. . . . God called the dry ground "land," and gathered waters he called "seas." And God saw that it was good. . . . The land produced vegetation. . . . And God saw that it was good. . . . God made two great lights. . . . God set them in the expanse of the sky. . . . And God saw that it was good. . . . God created the great creatures of the sea and every living and moving thing with which the water teems . . . and every winged bird. . . . And God saw that it was good. . . . God made the wild animals according to their kinds, the livestock according to their kinds, and all the creatures that move along the ground. . . . And God saw that it was good. (Genesis 1)

Good, *good*, GOOD! God saw that it was good! Six times in the first twenty-five verses the chorus of Genesis sounds its theme: "God saw that it was good."

Lynn White Jr. argued in his classic "Historical Roots" essay that

Christianity taught that all created things were made to serve human-kind,[25] that good means "good for us." There are many who think so. Their spokespersons include some of the world's best scholars. Where this road leads can be found in a book like *The Resourceful Earth: A Response to Global 2000,* edited by Julian Simon and the late Herman Kahn. For example, on the question of whether endangered species have value and whether we should save them, Simon and Kahn argue:

> We do not neglect the value of the passenger pigeon and other species that *may be valuable to us.* But we note that extinction of species—billions of them . . . has been a biological fact of life throughout the ages, just as has been the development of new species, some of which *may be more valuable to humans* than extinguished species whose niches they fill.[26] (emphasis ours)

These words are an excellent example of where that sort of thinking must inevitably end: in idolatry. The making of humanity into the measure of all use and value must, in the end, be accompanied by a blatant disregard for nonhuman life.

Though Lynn White's conclusions about the teachings of Genesis, that creation exists merely to serve humans, are not original, they still represent a mistaken exegesis of a magnificent text. At the time of God's pronouncements on the goodness of his creation, after God had ordered all things, no humans were yet present. Human beings are not created until the pronouncements are complete (Genesis 1:26), arriving as the last act of a nearly finished work. They are not asked to applaud, evaluate or critique. Their own opinion about creation's goodness is not considered and not solicited. The judgment has already been made, the valuation already declared, by the only Judge who really matters. Creation is good, in general and in particular, and its value exists because its Creator exists. It was brought into being to glorify God.

Of Leviathan and Behemoth

Not only does much of creation seem to have no *use* for humans (what use are frogs, toads, mice and fleas?), but some things appear to have been created precisely to be *useless* to us. Job's confrontation with God illustrates the point. Job asked why God had allowed misfortune to come to him. God does not directly answer the question, but draws

Job's attention to his creation, including the great sea monster Leviathan.

> Can you pull in the leviathan with a fishhook
> > or tie down his tongue with a rope?
> Can you put a cord through his nose
> > or pierce his jaw with a hook?
> Will he keep begging you for mercy?
> > Will he speak to you with gentle words?
> Will he make an agreement with you
> > for you to take him as your slave for life? . . .
> If you lay a hand on him,
> > you will remember the struggle and never do it again!
> Any hope of subduing him is false;
> > the mere sight of him is overpowering.
> No one is fierce enough to rouse him.
> > Who then is able to stand against me?
> Who has a claim against me that I must pay?
> > Everything under heaven belongs to me. (Job 41:1-4, 8-11)

God's point is that Job, a man, is not in a position to question whether God is fair, for God is the embodiment of fairness. Neither does God owe anyone anything, for all things belong to him, even the leviathan, over which Job has no control. Whatever God takes or gives are his own possessions. Some things exist, God implies, simply to display the splendor of God's act of creation:

> Look at the behemoth,
> > which I made along with you
> > and which feeds on grass like an ox.
> What strength he has in his loins,
> > what power in the muscles of his belly!
> His tail sways like a cedar;
> > the sinews of his thighs are close-knit.
> His bones are tubes of bronze,
> > his limbs like rods of iron.
> > He ranks first among the works of God. (Job 40:15-19)

God makes no offer to Job of a "useful" creation. He seems to take positive glee in pointing out how utterly and awesomely useless (to us) are some of the creatures he has made. "Nothing on earth," God concludes, "is [Leviathan's] equal—a creature without fear. He looks down on all that are haughty; he is king over all that are proud" (Job 41:33-34).

Leviathan and Behemoth are of no use to Job. They confound him. Yet God takes pleasure in them, and rightly so, for (among other reasons) they frustrate human wisdom, they destroy Job's (and our) illusion of control, that we are "masters of our fate and captains of our soul." To them God turns Job's attention, an appeal to know him for who he is, not who we think him to be, and so find the faith to trust in him again.

Some modern people think that all this has changed. They believe that through the achievements of modern science we can understand and control everything, or at least, we will someday. That is fortunately not the view of most practicing scientists, who know that the more they learn of their own field the less they truly understand it. The more arrogant view is that of people who learn their science from textbooks instead of from practice, and from a classroom instead of from life. God's response to Job is designed to help Job remove his focus from himself. God drives the point home in repeated lessons from creation. Who made the earth? Who enclosed the sea? Who made the flood? God brings to Job's mind the pride of his creation in animals—in the ostrich, the wild donkey, the horse and the hawk. In all these things, God reveals that he values his creation and is greatly pleased with it. And Job, for his part, has his focus restored. He no longer makes his own troubles the measure of God's fairness or of the universe's worth. "My ears had heard of you but now my eyes have seen you. Therefore I despise myself and repent in dust and ashes" (Job 42:5-6).

Job's fortunes were restored, and he lived to see better days than he had dreamed of. Will we? The essence of sin is for humans to make themselves, rather than God, the center of all things. This leads inevitably, wrote Bonhoeffer, to shame. "Instead of seeing God man sees himself."[27] Such shame leads to grief, and to a painful yet powerless longing to be restored. That is the problem that modern environmental ethics tries to address—that longing, the terrible sense of alienation from creation. But God himself is the only point at which such union can be achieved and a right perspective gained in life. One important evidence of that union is to hold a God-centered, or theocentric, value system in all things, including our relation to creation.

The Spirit of the Age

Sadly, much that passes for Christian writing in the present age does not share this biblical value system, but is blatantly anthropocentric and idolatrous. Yet God's truth, not contemporary Christian culture, must remain the measure of where true value lies. We can not only believe this but, in believing, also begin to experience the reality of it. It comes to us as the unspeakable, unnameable joy we know when we see creation's beauty *and* recognize the value that God gave it. At those moments we begin to see the goodness that God has made.

That joy, beauty and value can be argued about in academic discussions but are irrefutable in real life was revealed to me in an experience in southeastern Idaho. Our truck rounded a switchback on a mountain road in a misty predawn fog. Four other young men and I, all at that time employees of the U.S. Forest Service in the Salmon National Forest of Idaho, were headed for a remote area of the forest to plant trees. Without warning, and suddenly filling our entire windshield, a great golden eagle in flight was before us. He was only eight feet above the ground, with wings outstretched; his shadow covered the hood of our truck. Brakes screeched, bodies lurched forward. The magnificent creature turned effortlessly within three feet of the cab and soared down the mountainside, disappearing into the gray morning mists. Five human spectators gazed after, open-mouthed in wonder.

The linchpin of all ethical systems is the issue of value. If we fail to establish the real, inherent values in the things we are talking about, our efforts in ethics will be efforts in futility. And that is what secular systems of ethics are in regard to the environment. They struggle, but they cannot break free of the chains that bind them to humanity. Regardless of which human value is chosen, the ethical system ends up being anthropocentric. The inherent value of creation, the thing we feel so deeply and need so strongly, can be neither admitted nor addressed.

For many environmentalists, the mysticism of oneness with nature does address this deeply felt need. But if it succeeds where anthropocentric value systems fail, it fails where they have succeeded. It cannot articulate the inherent value of what we are seeking oneness with. What is the outcome? If an inherent value of creation is not recognized, it will ultimately be destroyed.

A case in point is the National Park Service. Fourteen national parks in North America have seen forty-two populations of mammals disappear. They are in danger of losing more. The reason? Many of our national parks, for all their beauty and value, were created primarily with human enjoyment in mind. Such parks were often too small to contain the intact ecosystems necessary to the survival of large mobile mammals. In addition, the Park Service has vacillated between managing the parks for people and managing them for creation. Traditionally, people have won out. In some cases, like Yellowstone, park rangers themselves took an active part in exterminating certain species of large mammals from the park. The parks often have been managed to maximize human use. As a result, many species of animals are gone.[28]

Sustaining Creation

The high mountains belong to the wild goats;
    the crags are a refuge for the coneys. . . .
These all look to you
    to give them their food at the proper time.
When you give it to them,
    they gather it up;
when you open your hand,
    they are satisfied with good things.
When you hide your face,
    they are terrified;
When you take away their breath,
    they die and return to the dust.
When you send your Spirit,
    they are created;
    and you renew the face of the earth. (Psalm 104:18, 27-30)

God is intimately involved in his creation because he values it. He not only made it but also sustains it. This too is part of creation's value, for creation did not make itself, nor does it sustain itself. The value God imparts to creation by his care demands that the creation around us be not merely preserved but also restored, reflecting the plants and animals that once lived on a site before human use overruled them.

Scripture provides a logical value system. It establishes that the whole creation in general, and every part of it in particular, has a value given to it by God. This does not mean that the creation is *inherently* good or that it has a right to exist on its own merits, independent of God. Its goodness is derived from its Creator and so is a kind of "grace" goodness, freely given in love, not grudgingly merited by right.

Indeed, the Bible has precious little to say about rights, for humans or for creation. The biblical writers were much more interested, indeed, enthralled, with other concepts, like love, mercy and grace. As one of C. S. Lewis's characters says in *The Great Divorce*, "I haven't got my rights or I should not be here. You will not get yours either. You'll get something far better. Never fear."[29]

And creation will get something far better too. Never fear. Not its rights, but its hopes. Not its due, but its longing. For God never merely fulfills duties. He accomplishes dreams. "The creation waits in eager expectation for the sons of God to be revealed" (Romans 8:19).

That value and that hope make up the story we have not heard, yet long to hear again. They are the shadow of the vision we cannot recognize, yet strain to see. They are the echo of the song we have forgotten, yet long to sing again. But how can we answer a call we do not understand?

Once we did. Once we knew how to answer. "The LORD God had formed out of the ground all the beasts of the field and all the birds of the air. He brought them to the man to see what he would name them; and whatever the man called each living creature, that was its name" (Genesis 2:19).

Can you name what you do not value? Can you name a child that is not yours? That which we know and treasure and love we name. And that which we name knows us. So once humans did not fear God's creatures, and they did not fear humankind. Man named them and knew their value. But human beings participated in the joy of creation in another way as well, not only in naming but in keeping: "A river watering the garden flowed from Eden; from there it was separated into four headwaters. . . . The LORD God took the man and put him in the Garden of Eden to work it and take care of it" (Genesis 2:10, 15).

Here, even more directly, man participates in the will of God and in the life of creation. Just as loving is better than mere knowing, so caring is better than mere naming. Not out of need, but out of love, God chooses to involve us in the care of creation. But all that has changed, and it is the bitterest of tragedies.

The man said, "The woman you put here with me—she gave me some fruit from the tree, and I ate it." . . .

[God answered:] "Cursed is the ground because of you;
through painful toil you will eat of it all the days of your life.
It will produce thorns and thistles for you,
and you will eat the plants of the field.
By the sweat of your brow
you will eat your food
until you return to the ground,
since from it you were taken;
for dust you are,
and to dust you will return." (Genesis 3:12, 17-19)

And so we lost our recognition of creation's value, and became the agents of creation's curse. More must be said of this elsewhere. But it was the end of Eden. And of all the stories ever told, that is the saddest one we know.

We all long to participate in that value again, to be needed and noticed by creation. When I lived in the urban Midwest and life in the city sometimes became more than I could bear, I would go to the forests of northern lower Michigan in the Au Sable River region, especially in October, when the landscape glowed in the blush of yellow, red and gold. The beauty of today's forests I owe to the sugar maples, which have grown up in the last seventy years. But the earlier glory of the Au Sable I shall never see; no one will ever see again the great stands of 150-foot-high white and red pines, stretching ridge upon ridge and valley to valley. Au Sable, you are precious to me, but the grandeur of your elder forests I shall never know, all because we gave you no value but board feet and saw logs, no use but a house and a chair and a board and a bed. And now the greater glories of Eden are gone forever.

I do not now live near the Au Sable River. There are days when the memories of it and the longing for it are painful. But deep within the human spirit, all of us long for a day of living in and being part of something we were separated from long ago. We can begin the road back through a knowledge of God the Creator, and by a rediscovery of the value which he gave to his creation.

Questions for Thought and Discussion
1. How is creation's value to God different from other ways of giving value to creation?

2. How do we know that creation's value exists independently of its usefulness and utility to humans?

3. How would you demonstrate to others in daily life that you believe creation is both valuable and good?

4. How would you use or enjoy creation in ways that gain values from it that are similar to values God gains from it?

4
Out of the Dust

Man is a mediator. He is poised between two
realities: God and the world. He shares in
both, he is united to both. He cannot live
apart from either. That is the meaning of the
incarnation of Jesus Christ.
P A U L O S   G R E G O R I O S [1]

I N THE BEGINNING GOD CREATED THE HEAVENS AND THE EARTH"
(Genesis 1:1). So the Bible opens its revelation to us with this first
statement of Genesis. Christians commonly refer to the Bible as
"God's Word," and this is appropriate. From first to last, God is Scripture's dominant subject. As Derek Kidner noted, "This passage, indeed
the Book, is about him [God] first of all; to read it with any other
primary interest is to misread it."[2]

It is critical that we not miss the significance of the Bible's opening
statement. It is a statement that stands in marked contrast to the myths
of Israel's neighboring cultures. Their gods were many, and in both
form and attributes were very much a part of this world. But the God
of Israel begins by declaring not only his power but his transcendence.
Only he creates free and distinct from the world. Only he gives to each
thing its original form and being, yet he himself owes nothing to
anything.[3]

God's creative ability is different from the creative ability we have.
We may create many things with hand and tool and mind, but they are
always limited. The Creator speaks and it is done. In face of this we are
both reassured and frightened at the same moment. We can only say
with Scripture, "You alone are holy" (Revelation 15:4).

In Genesis, God's final act of creation is to bring forth humanity. The significance of this act is indicated by the phrase "let us make" (Genesis 1:26) in contrast to "let the land produce" (Genesis 1:24), the phrase used to describe the creation of plants and animals. The divine self-community proclaims a momentous step. When God brings forth a creature made in his own image, the creation is complete.[4]

The creation exists solely because of the will and acts of God. And we, as humans, are linked to all other created things by our Creator. But this is only the beginning of the links that bind us to the cosmos.

The Linkage of Substance

As a college professor, sometimes I would take small groups of students away from the concrete of the campus and into the living world of the forest. I remember a trip to one place called Fogwell Forest, only a few minutes' drive from campus. It was small, about twenty-eight acres. It was an "unadvertised" preserve. Few visited it. It had no billboards to direct the curious, no trails to aid the novice.

We made our way to Fogwell as best we could. As we walked toward the forest through a soybean field, we began taking measurements. It was early October, and air and soil temperature in the field were about 70 degrees, humidity 59 percent. Among the soybeans, incident light reaching the ground was one thousand footcandles per square meter. The soil pH, a measure of its acidity, was 4.0, more than ten times the acidity of normal rainwater.

As we entered the forest we continued measuring. Though small, Fogwell was considered worth preserving because it was one of the last stands of old-growth, river-bottom forest communities in this part of the country. As we went in, we noted a series of remarkable changes. Only fifty yards into the woods, air temperature had dropped to 58 degrees and soil temperature to 54. Humidity rose dramatically to 71 percent. The pH increased to 7.0, a neutral, or balanced, pH like that of distilled water. The canopy, rising up to eighty to one hundred feet above our heads on the tops of hundred-year-old beeches and maples, was allowing only forty footcandles of light per square meter to reach the surface.

I asked my students, "Why these sudden and dramatic changes as we go from soybeans to sugar maples?" They concluded, correctly, that the canopy's shading had drastically reduced air and soil temperature as well as incoming light. The plants' release of water into the air through their leaves, a process called transpiration, raised the humidity around us. Decomposing plant material on the ground buffered the forest soil better than the artificially fertilized soybean field, moving the soil pH toward a more neutral point, better for growing plants.

I ask a second question: "Are these changes a cause of the forest's occurrence or an effect of it?" The answer escapes no one. These dramatic changes are effects generated, in part, by the forest itself. The life of the forest in turn contributes to an environment favorable to the forest. And the linkage of sun, air, plant and soil are one.

I turn over a log. Millipedes, ants, termites, a centipede and a salamander scuttle away for dear life. Another question must be asked. "Where does the debris from this rotting log end and the soil begin?" Half a dozen pairs of hands begin scraping, like pirates for a treasure chest, to find the answer. But it eludes us. Slowly, imperceptibly, there is less and less log and more and more soil.

I decide to get more precise. A soil sampling tube is brought forth, pushed deep into the ground, then withdrawn. At the top it is filled with decaying pieces of litter, mostly from the rotting log. Looking deeper, we see that the decaying matter becomes more broken up, but still abundant, rich and black. In another four inches it begins to lighten to dark brown, then brownish red. By the bottom of the tube, even the consistency has changed. From the rich, black mulch on the surface, the bottom yields a slimy red clay. And the students and I now understand yet another linkage. Just as the forest helps to create its own environment, it also builds its own soil, and builds it from the dead, decaying bodies of what were once some of its most prominent citizens. In the forest, the death of one generation is the life of the next. Like soil forming under logs, one merges imperceptibly with the other.

My work is over now. I sit on the banks of a river not far from my home. It meanders slowly northward, oozing along through the city, slow and thick and brown like cheap pancake syrup. I am only a few feet above the water, but I cannot see into it. The silt load is too high. The river carries away the soil from the corn and soybean fields planted to its edge. And so the forest is cut, and the rains come. The crops grow, and the soil washes away. And the river carries away the links that we have broken, the land and soil we have despised.

God created the universe in such a way that humans are inseparably linked to it, physically as well as spiritually. Out of the common stuff of earth God formed a man. "The LORD God formed the man from the dust of the ground, and breathed into his nostrils the breath of life, and the man became a living being" (Genesis 2:7).

Recognizing our finiteness, we acknowledge our linkage to creation in a common Creator. We are also linked in substance. We are not, in that substance, fundamentally different from other life. We are not made of some special, ethereal matter that is different from that of a moose or a frog or an insect. The same potassium, nitrogen, carbon, oxygen, hydrogen and other elements found in other living things, and in nonliving matter, are found in us. Our very genetic identity, our DNA, contains the same elements as that of every other living creature. The substance of the earth itself is basic to our makeup.

We did not require science to tell us this, but it has confirmed the Scripture's witness, a story of a man made "from the dust of the ground," just as the animals are formed "out of the ground." The Hebrew word *'ādam* may be used as a proper name, but it can, in its broadest sense, mean "man" or "mankind." The Hebrew word *"dāmâh* means earth or dust of the earth. As Loren Wilkinson noted, "It is as though the biblical writer declared that God made humans out of humus."[5]

Our pride may be repulsed at this thought. We often cultivate feelings of separation and distinction from the rest of creation. Such separation can be especially acute when we spend most of our time in environments of our own making, in heated buildings and air-conditioned cars. The Teacher of Ecclesiastes offers a different, and clearer, perspective. "As for men, God tests them so that they may see that they are like the animals. Man's fate is like that of the animals; the same fate awaits them both: As one dies, so dies the other. All have the same breath. . . . All go to the same place; all come from dust, and to dust all return" (Ecclesiastes 3:18-20). The Bible makes clear that many dimensions of our existence will not end with death. But our physical life is linked, from beginning to end, to the life of the world, through the soil of the earth.

Before the communist revolution in Ethiopia, then-emperor Haile

Selassie made a state visit to Egypt. While there he walked to the edge of the Nile and scooped up two handfuls of mud from its banks. Raising his hands, he exclaimed, "My country."[6] Those things that people value most—order, peace, food and freedom—all washed away in the mud of the Nile, and famine and revolution took their place. The work of our hands and the institutions of government, those things we most want to attribute to human ingenuity, are in fact inseparably tied to the creation around us.

Because all creation shares a common substance, all creation brings its Creator praise. So "the heavens declare the glory of God" (Psalm 19:1), as do the lilies of the field, clothed in "splendor" (Luke 12:27-28), and the sea monster Leviathan, a "creature without fear" (Job 41:33). As theologian Joseph Sittler said, "Nature comes from God, cannot be apart from God, and is capable of beaming the glory of God."[7] Our own praise to God is part of creation's chorus.

Blessing

As God created us and made us with a common substance, he bestowed on all creatures a common blessing. Not only humans but all creatures are blessed by God to be fruitful and multiply (Genesis 1:22).

This blessing reveals three things. First, it signifies God's generosity. God does not have to create anything, yet he does. "How many are your works, O LORD! In wisdom you made them all; the earth is full of your creatures" (Psalm 104:24). To affirm the generosity of God is to celebrate creation as a gift. And it is to know ourselves, with all creation, as recipients in divine beneficence.

Second, to affirm the blessedness of creation is to affirm an independent source of its worth and value—God. Because "God so loved the world" (John 3:16), all created things have value. The book of Job describes God's merciful (and impartial) care for all his creatures. Job asks God to answer the riddle of his unmerited suffering. God's answer is to focus Job's attention on his mysterious yet all-encompassing care of every living thing. In a culture obsessed with itself, God would turn our focus to the same things today.

Third, it is by God's blessing that creation exists and continues to exist, and it is that blessing of existence that allows the creature to be freely and completely itself before its Creator. God gives his creatures integrity, and with that the fruitfulness inherent in all life. All beings share something of the divine nature and creativity in their ability to reproduce (Genesis 1:22). Life on earth flourishes because of the Creator's blessing.

But blessing is not one-dimensional or one-way. It also can flow from created things to their Creator. By carrying out our designated roles on earth, we bless the One who made us (Psalm 115:16-18), as do other creatures (Psalm 145:21). And when we do, we can understand, for ourselves as well as for other creatures, what Francis of Assisi meant by his words to the famous hymn, "Let all things their Creator bless, and worship him in humbleness." Our lives take on new dimension and meaning when we realize that we can, through them, give blessing to the God who made the cosmos.

In saying this, we are consciously rejecting an idea which has grown stronger in Western churches with each passing year—that what is spiritual is more valuable and more important than what is physical. In this view, the world is a threat and a source of contamination from which Christians must escape. Behind this view lies the ancient gnostic heresy that only the abstract, the idea, is the true being. Matter and reality are illusions. To hold such a view is to deny a truth which the Bible plainly teaches, the linkage between ourselves and creation.

Shalom

All creation shares the shalom of God. *Shalom* is a Hebrew word that expresses God's perfect will for creation. While it is often translated as "peace," the term contains a greater depth of meaning than we usually appreciate. Shalom is a powerful Old Testament concept expressing wholeness and well-being. Because the author of shalom is God, shalom is associated with "love and faithfulness . . . righteousness and peace" (Psalm 85:10). It is the opposite of wickedness, where "there is no peace" (Isaiah 57:21).[8] Shalom is more than simply the absence of hostility. It is more than even being in right relationship. In its highest sense, shalom implies finding joy and pleasure in every relationship. As Nicholas Wolterstorff has said, "Shalom is perfected when humanity acknowledges that in its service of God is true delight."[9]

The Genesis account of creation is a picture of the universe in shalom: a cosmos of peace, order, well-being and joy. Where shalom reigns, all exist in right relation to one another and to their Creator. Theologian Walter Brueggemann has reflected on this and said, "The central theme of world history in the Bible is that all creation is one, living in harmony and security toward the joy and well-being of every other creature."[10]

Sin

The world was created in the harmony of shalom, but it no longer exists in it. Being made in God's image, humans were created as God's designated representatives on the earth. The psalmist writes, "You made him ruler over the works of your hands; you put everything under his feet" (Psalm 8:6). At God's command, humans are involved in the creative process in the naming of other creatures. No other living thing is given these responsibilities.

Such responsibilities can only exist in the freedom of choice. If something is capable of being truly good, it must also be capable of being truly bad. Otherwise its goodness is merely instinctive behavior. So a bad man can be far worse than a bad horse. Choice is the joy and sorrow of being human. God does not hesitate to address us as creatures who make choices. "I have set before you life and death, blessings and curses. Now choose life, so that you and your children may live, and that you may love the LORD your God, listen to his voice, and hold fast to him." (Deuteronomy 30:19-20). Our freedom of choice is experienced as a constant struggle between good and evil. And our choices have cosmic consequences.

In direct disobedience to God, Adam and Eve eat fruit from a tree they are specifically told not to touch. It is the biblical view that this single event is the key to understanding all the evil and human failure in the world, and the key to understanding human nature itself. It is through this act that we became what we are. As Paul says, "Through the disobedience of the one man the many were made sinners" (Romans 5:19). In a desire for illegitimate authority, in a desire to "be like God" (Genesis 3:5), Adam and Eve rebelled against their Creator. The same sin results in our lives as we choose to continue our part in their revolt.

Failure to recognize this part and parcel of human nature is what leads to the bewilderment, and eventual failure, of secular systems of environmental ethics. Over forty years ago Aldo Leopold wrote despairingly, "In many parts of Mexico, South America, South Africa, and Australia a violent and accelerating wastage is in progress, but I cannot yet assess the prospects."[11] Today we can assess the prospects there and elsewhere, and they are well summarized by the historian Lynn White Jr.: "More science and more technology are not going to get us out of the current ecological crisis."[12] Quite right. The sinful nature of humanity is nowhere more evident in a world in which we possess the means to care for creation but not the will. And to admit this is one of the most penetrating and painful confessions that an unbelieving world can make. Yet the facts force this admission upon us.

To this dilemma, the Word of God speaks. Its voice is painful. First, it correctly identifies all sin as, at base, directed against God. David understood this when he wrote, "Against you, you only, have I sinned" (Psalm 51:4). Whether by omission or commission, whether by willful trespass or careless negligence, sin is fully recognized as evil because it is ultimately directed against God and contradicts all that characterizes a holy Creator.

If the voice of God's Word is painful, it also speaks in mercy, for it tells us the truth, and in that truth provides an answer and a hope. The Bible correctly reveals that sin expresses itself relationally, that is, through the breaking of relationships on many different levels. The force of sin in the world disrupts four basic relationships: the relation of human beings to God, the relation of a person to herself or himself, the relations of people to one another, and the relation of humanity to creation. It is this fourth disruption which concerns us here.

Judgment
This "fall of man" is not a theological abstract. It had and continues to have profound implications. Uniquely delegated as God's representatives, humans were placed in a creation which had been made to be responsive to them. That would no longer be so. Now it became a struggle to live in creation, and a strenuous effort to carry out God-given responsibilities. Instead of seeking God, Adam and Eve hide from him (Genesis 3:8). Shame and fear become their dominant emotions, even as they dominate human nature today. God's response to their rebellion was reproof, condemnation, curse and expulsion from their previously perfect world.

Not only humanity but the world around it was changed, and creation came under God's curse through human disobedience. "Cursed is the ground because of you," said God. "It will produce thorns and thistles for you. . . . By the sweat of your brow you will eat your food." (Genesis 3:17-19). Instead of harmony, there is brokenness. As Henri Blocher has said, "If man obeyed God, he would be the means of blessing the earth; but in his insatiable greed, in his scorn for the balances built into the created order and in his short-sightedness he pollutes and destroys it. He turns a garden into a desert (Revelation 11:18). That is the main thrust of the curse of Genesis."[13]

This does not mean that any created thing is evil. It is the witness of both the Old (Genesis 1) and New Testaments (1 Timothy 4:4) that "everything God created is good." But the ground expresses its curse in that we are set against it. What was once a garden whose nature was to produce fruit is now a briar patch that can yield food only with backbreaking labor. Creatures we once named now flee from us in terror or try to do us harm. Our actions toward creation are henceforth always frustrated because of our sin, even when we try to do good. On a small scale we see this in the loss of entire communities of creatures, like the tall-grass prairie of the United States or the tropical dry forest of Central America.

I can still recall my first airplane ride, not because of any fear from being so far above the ground but because it provided my first real glimpse of the profound changes that humans have produced on the earth. From the air, I could begin to see that the woodlots and wetlands that I loved so much were only tiny islands in a sea of farms and cities. Eastern North America's vast forests of presettlement times are now largely gone. Later plane rides revealed to me that there are still vast areas of our world, and even the United States, that show no sign of human presence. The mountain goats that dash headlong down the cliffs of the Line Creek Canyon and the elk that rest in the summer sedge meadows on the Silver Run Plateau in Montana still live as ever did the goats and elk that bore them. But these too are shrinking islands in a raging sea of change. Severe and permanent alteration of the earth is the rule of our age. Not every change is evil, but the human will to place its own needs above those of God's other creatures is often terrible, and illustrates how the idolatry prohibited by the first and second commandments can express itself (Exodus 20:2-3).

The Bible never treats sin as a merely spiritual phenomenon. Isaiah proclaims that the earth is defiled under its inhabitants because they break the laws of God (Isaiah 24:5). The failure to obey God's laws not only led to Israel's captivity and exile, but devastated the entire land. The prophet Hosea, speaking for God, told the people of Israel that their evil affected every living thing: "There is no faithfulness, no love, no acknowledgment of God in the land. . . . Because of this the land mourns, and all who live in it waste away; the beasts of the field and the birds of the air and the fish of the sea are dying" (Hosea 4:1, 3).

The physical effects of this disharmony between God, humanity and creation are well documented. Palestinian explorer John Currid wrote, "In the ancient Near East . . . the deforestation of major tracts of land was not primarily due to natural causes, but rather to the ravages of man."[14] Dennis Baly, author of *The Geography of the Bible,* commented, "Thousands of years ago, the soil was thick enough for cultivation or for the growth of forests over much larger areas in the hills than at present, but the work of destruction, so long continued, has meant that . . . in many places the soil is no longer there."[15] Even at the beginning of the twentieth century, George Adam Smith, an explorer and frequent visitor to Palestine, described Israel as a land that had "been stripped and starved, its bones protrude, in places it is very bald—a carcass of a land, if you like . . . and especially when the clouds lower, or the sirocco throws dust across the sun."[16]

These testimonies of God and men, undeniably accurate as they are, do not sound very hopeful. Yet we said that the Scripture spoke of hope. So it does. In contrast to this despair, there are frequent references to a time when shalom would prevail again as it did in Eden. Redemption accomplished by God would bring a new order and nature to the world (Isaiah 11:6-10; 55:12-13) in which peace and harmony would prevail. The fulfillment of this hope depended on the coming of God, the Messiah (Isaiah 9:6-7).

The New Testament is a witness to how this hope came and is coming to be fulfilled through Jesus Christ (Luke 1:79; 2:14). Through him peace comes and shalom is bestowed (Mark 5:34; John 20:19, 21, 26). His disciples are its messengers (Luke 10:5-11, 16; Acts 10:36). Jesus himself is the Prince of Peace, redeeming the world to himself (Isaiah 9:6).

Though the total well-being of the world is still ahead, those who follow Christ are called to prepare the world for it. Today there is much emphasis on this preparation in spiritual things, to be made right with God on earth and enjoy his shalom in heaven. But Paul describes all creation waiting "in eager expectation for the sons of God to be revealed" (Romans 8:19). As children of God, Christians are to begin restoring shalom to creation, expectantly looking, with creation, for the completeness of it in God's kingdom to come.

Throughout the Scriptures the visions of the kingdom of God are visions of humanity in harmony with creation. Theologian Ralph Smith observes, "If biblical man did not foresee a time when man would have no need of nature, perhaps modern man should begin to make his peace with it now."[17]

Preservation

In spite of sin and judgment, God has chosen to preserve creation. We, as humans, are linked to all other creatures in that preservation. As Dietrich Bonhoeffer noted, those who speak of a "continual creation" ignore the reality of the Fall. What is around us today is not creation remade but creation preserved. In spite of sin, it does not sink back into chaos and void. And in that preservation, we understand that the world is not preserved for its own sake, but for the sake of the sight of God. And this preservation is God's testimony that creation is still good in his sight.[18]

Our linkage to creation in preservation is dramatically illustrated in the ark (Genesis 6:14). From listening to the emphasis of modern sermons, one would get the impression that the ark was constructed solely to preserve some representatives of humanity (Noah and his family). If that had been God's sole purpose, a rowboat and some umbrellas would have sufficed. The ark is constructed specifically to preserve creation (Genesis 6:19-21). In this we see the flood's paradox. We are linked to creation in judgment, and both the human and the nonhuman are destroyed in God's verdict against evil. But we also are linked to creation in preservation, and both the human and the nonhuman are preserved. In the words of the apostle Paul, "Consider therefore the kindness and sternness of God" (Romans 11:22).

In seeing God's preservation, we understand the importance of preservation as one aspect of service to God on earth. It is not the only aspect, and, as we shall see in chapter five, something better than mere preservation awaits both us and creation. But if we would represent God in and to a fallen world, preservation of his created order is one of our tasks now.

Sabbath

In creation, God's work is sealed with the words "He rested" (Genesis 2:3). This brief statement is the key to understanding a vital concept that links us to him and to his creation. This is the concept of sabbath. God does not rest from fatigue, but in enjoyment of finished achievement. His rest is not inactivity, for he continues to nurture what he creates. The New Testament speaks of this rest as Jesus "seated" after his finished work of redemption in order to give to others the benefits of his work (Hebrews 8:1; 10:12). Likewise, the New Testament gives a call to all Christians to make this rest a part of their own lives, and enter into it through faith in Christ (Hebrews 4:1). To observe the sabbath is for all the created order to recognize that it came from God and belongs to him forever, the recipient of his blessing. That is why God's laws concerning the sabbath were never confined to people, but explicitly included animals and the land itself.

Trophime Mouiren, in his book *The Creation*, says, "The creation has no meaning for man unless man takes time to give it meaning in rest and prayer: rest, in order to look at the word otherwise than simply as answering his needs; prayer, to ask God's blessings, to offer something to God."[19]

We have diluted the idea of sabbath today. Even among Christians, if they observe it at all, the sabbath is only a symbol of belonging to God and a recuperative experience. We understand sabbath better if we consider the thoughts of David Ehrenfeld, an Orthodox Jew who also happens to be a professor of ecology. Ehrenfeld notes that an observant Jew would observe the sabbath by more than resting, praying and refraining from ordinary work. Three other aspects are carefully followed: creating nothing, destroying nothing and enjoying the bounty of the earth. To be careful that nothing is created reminds us that God is the supreme Creator. To be careful that nothing is destroyed reminds us that the world is God's creation, and not our possession to ruin. To enjoy the earth's bounty reminds us that God, not human invention, is the source of that bounty.[20] This is a richer, fuller sabbath tradition based on biblical witness. It should disturb us that these thoughts are so foreign to Christians today.

As we noted, the observance of sabbath applies to the treatment of land, and of our relationship to the owner and creator of that land. "The land," God tells Moses, ". . . must observe a sabbath to the LORD" (Leviticus 25:1). He explains further that the land must rest every seventh year. In that year no fields are to be plowed, no crops cultivated.

Part of the purpose of this observance was to teach God's people greater faith in him (Leviticus 25), but the practice also has significant ecological justification. Allowing land to lie fallow helps to restore depleted fertility and can reduce erosion, if it is properly treated beforehand. An even more radical observance was demanded by God in the year after the seventh sabbath (every fiftieth year). This was the year of Jubilee. In this "sabbath of sabbaths" (Leviticus 25) not only was land not to be cultivated, but property was reverted to its original owner, debts were forgiven and slaves were set free. Thus God intended that large blocks of land and large amounts of money would not be concentrated in the hands of a wealthy few, nor would slavery be a permanent part of any Israelite's life. Indeed, the intention of both sabbath and Jubilee was meant to begin to reverse the curse of Genesis. Instead of bread by the sweat of their face, people would eat the bounty of the previous year (which God promised to provide) at rest. And land management would be made responsible to the real owner in gratitude. For, as God reminded the Israelites in observing these laws, they were strangers and sojourners in the land—tenants, not owners.

Thus the Bible teaches a concept of sabbath much broader than most people today would make it. We are called to keep the sabbath not only personally but also for the land and for its other inhabitants. Our motive is to demonstrate love and obedience to God, the Creator and owner of all, and so to affirm our lasting linkage both with him and with his creation.

The Separations of Sin and Judgment
The Fall is always treated by Scripture as an actual historic event, an event which came through a deliberate and willful human decision to

disobey God. This event led to four great separations.

First came a separation of humans from God. "I heard you in the garden, and I was afraid," said Adam. The Fall changed the joy of fellowship with God into a relationship of fear, and a life of futility in which human beings try to hide from God in the midst of his own creation.

Second, the Fall created a separation of human beings from each other. "The woman you put here with me—she gave me some fruit from the tree," says Adam. He describes Eve, a creature he once marveled at in joy, without even calling her by name. So begins humanity's long practice of blame-shifting. "It's her fault for giving me the fruit," Adam implies, "and it's your fault, God, for giving her to me." Thus a relationship meant to visibly demonstrate unity becomes only another casualty of division.

Third, each human became divided in and separated from the self. "I was afraid because I was naked," says Adam. He felt not only physically naked (that was the state in which he was created) but spiritually naked as well. Adam realizes too late that his own soul has been stripped of its holiness and that a direct approach to God is now no longer possible, or even desirable.

Fourth, humans were separated from creation. "The LORD God banished him from the Garden. . . . He drove the man out" (Genesis 3:23). Human beings, designed to productively preserve and cultivate the world with the blessing of God, encountered futility in every day's experience, and Adam's best efforts were just enough to sustain him, no more. "Cursed is the ground because of you," God says to Adam. "Through painful toil you will eat of it all the days of your life. It will produce thorns and thistles for you, and you will eat the plants of the field. By the sweat of your brow you will eat your food, until you return to the ground, since from it you were taken; for dust you are, and to dust you will return" (Genesis 3:17-19).

It is this last division, this great division between humanity and creation, that concerns us here. Through acts of preservation in the midst of judgment, through the promise and experience of sabbath and shalom, which are foretastes of a peace with creation and with God that seem impossible to recapture, both humanity and creation begin to see and feel their desperate need of a Redeemer, and of a redemption sufficient to heal what sin has made impossible for them to restore.

Questions for Thought and Discussion

1. What evidence does Genesis 3 provide that sin involves more than personal disobedience to God? In what ways does sin affect all of the creation?

2. What effects of the separation between humanity and creation described in the Bible have you seen in your own experience? Is there any way these effects could be undone?

3. In what ways do you or could you deliberately practice a greater experience of sabbath and shalom with God? In what ways could you encourage your church to do this?

5
Covenant & Redemption

We did not inherit the land from our fathers.
We are borrowing it from our children.
A M I S H   P R O V E R B

I N THE THIRD CHAPTER OF GENESIS THE BIBLE DESCRIBES THE FALL OF humanity, how we gained the knowledge of good and evil and so were driven out of Eden. The words here tell of more than a removal of two human beings from a physical place, but of a deep division that has been made between humanity and creation.

"Cursed is the ground because of you," God said to Adam. "Through painful toil you will eat of it all the days of your life. It will produce thorns and thistles for you, and you will eat the plants of the field. By the sweat of your brow you will eat your food, until you return to the ground, since from it you were taken; for dust you are, and to dust you will return" (Genesis 3:17-19). It is only in attention to this story, and of what follows after, that we can hope to understand the needs of creation and its hopes, both entwined in our needs and hopes—the promise of covenant and of redemption.

"With curse and promise," wrote Dietrich Bonhoeffer, "God speaks to the fallen, unreconciled, fleeing Adam. Adam is preserved alive in a world between curse and promise, and the last promise is the permission to die. Paradise is destroyed."[1]

Covenant

It is in this world—a creation and a humanity between curse and promise—that God established his covenant. *Covenant* is not a commonly used word today. Its dictionary definition is "a binding agreement between two or more persons or parties, a contract or compact."[2] When the term is used by God, its meaning takes on greater and deeper dimensions. It is a sovereign dispensing of grace or undeserved favor on his part, and the security of the relationship established arises from the actions of God.

For example, God blessed Noah and told him,

I now establish my covenant with you and with your descendants after you and with every living creature that was with you—the birds, the livestock and all the wild animals, all those that came out of the ark with you—every living creature on earth. I establish my covenant with you: Never again will all life be cut off by the waters of a flood. Never again will there be a flood to destroy the earth. (Genesis 9:8-11)

As a perpetual reminder of this covenant, God chose a dramatic visual symbol.

I have set my rainbow in the clouds, and it will be the sign of the covenant between me and the earth. Whenever I bring clouds over the earth and the rainbow appears in the clouds, I will remember my covenant between me and you and all living creatures of every kind. Never again will the waters become a flood to destroy all life. (Genesis 9:13-15)

So a permanent, recurring seal is set in creation to proclaim God's promise, and the agent of judgment (rain) is always followed by the promise of preservation.

These words describe what theologians typically call the Noachian covenant. But it could just as well, indeed more properly, be called the Creation covenant, for it is part of God's determination to preserve (as discussed in chapter four) and ultimately redeem creation. Throughout this covenant, God repeatedly affirms that it is a promise not merely to Noah but to "every living creature on earth." Noah acts as creation's representative, but the promise of God is given to all creatures and to the earth itself:

As long as the earth endures,

seedtime and harvest,
cold and heat,
summer and winter,
day and night
will never cease. (Genesis 8:22)

The forceful assurance of this covenant should not be missed. The eleventh verse of chapter nine contains a double negative. "Never again will all life be cut off by a waters of the flood; never again will there again be a flood to destroy the earth." Such a double negative in Hebrew contains a much stronger and more emotional statement than equivalent English expressions can convey. It is the sense of "No, no, never again!"

This covenant has five important features: (1) It is conceived and established by God. (2) Its scope is universal, embracing all creation under God's care and protection. (3) It is unconditional, without requiring merit on the part of Noah or any other living thing. (4) It shall last as long as the earth remains. (5) And its satisfaction hinges only on the Creator's beneficence. In all these things, the covenant is ordained and completed by God through grace. Its fulfillment does not depend on the beneficiaries' understanding, for how does the sparrow understand God's care (Luke 12:6)? Likewise, the beneficiaries can do nothing to earn the covenant's benefits, nor instruct God as to the execution of its provisions. For "who has known the mind of the Lord? Or who has been his counselor?" (Romans 11:34).

It is tragic that, in an age in which the church prides itself on the sophistication of its Sunday-school curriculum, the story of Noah is one which adult Christians are taught to outgrow. While paper giraffes and hippopotamuses in cardboard arks amuse those in the nursery, older Christians are allowed to forget the greatness of God's promise, symbolized by the rainbow.

In John's Revelation, the rainbow again symbolizes this covenant with creation. "At once I was in the Spirit, and there before me was a throne in heaven with someone sitting on it. And the one who sat there had the appearance of jasper and carnelian. A rainbow, resembling an emerald, encircled the throne" (Revelation 4:2-3). Of this vision, theologian G. R. Beasley-Murray wrote, "The object of the rainbow is primarily to conceal the form of God; yet it is significant that a rainbow and not an ordinary cloud perform this service, for the bow is a perpetual reminder of God's covenant to restrain His wrath from men on earth (Genesis 9:13). The memorial of the covenant in heaven is thus nothing less than the glory of God which hides Him from angelic view."[3] So it is that God has sealed this covenant between himself and creation with the personal symbol of his own presence, placing himself between us and his wrath against our evil.

An understanding of this covenant is of more than historical or theological interest. It is foundational to understanding an authentic value for the life that God has placed in the world, and of his determination to preserve it.

A Modern Debate

In the January 1989 issue of the professional scientific journal *Bio-Science*, a short debate was published between Norman Levine, professor emeritus of veterinary medicine at the University of Illinois, and Norman Myers, an eminent world authority on conservation and problems of endangered species. Levine argued that any attempt to save endangered species was a waste of time and resources: "Extinction is an inevitable fact of evolution, and it is needed for progress. New species continually arise, and they are better adapted to their environment than those that have died out."[4] From this Levine concluded, "Evolution exists, and it goes on continually. People are here because of it, but people may be replaced someday. It is neither possible nor desirable to stop it, and that is what we are trying to do when we try to preserve species on their way out."[5]

Myers, for his part, argued that present extinctions are cause for concern because they are occurring faster than former ones. "In the longer term," wrote Myers, "there will surely be an unprecedented slowing down of speciation insofar as certain creative capacities of evolution will be diminished."[6] This loss of biodiversity, Myers argues, will undoubtedly impoverish the evolutionary process in future generations.

Myers makes a second argument for saving endangered species. Such species, he asserts, may one day serve human needs and provide valuable resources if their populations can be restored to levels large enough to permit exploitation. He offers the example of the endangered golden tamarin monkey (actually a marmoset) of South America. Its relative, the cotton-topped marmoset, has proved "an unusually suitable model for cancer research." Myers asks, "Who knows what medical benefits might be available from the tamarin?"[7]

Both men ask an important question: What is the value of (and reason for) saving endangered species? Therefore their arguments deserve analysis. Levine argues that, because evolution has occurred in the past, and is now occurring, it should continue to occur ("should," in the sense that Levine uses it, seems to mean "it is desirable"). It is not present life, or even human life, to which Levine assigns the highest value ("people are here because of it [evolution], but people may be replaced someday"). It is the process of evolution itself. And since Levine feels that his own destiny, as well as that of his species, is controlled by evolution, he is willing to accept its outcomes without question and call them good. Like the physicist Weston in C. S. Lewis's novel *Out of the Silent Planet,* Levine does not know what will happen in the course of evolution, but he hopes it will happen very much. In Levine's view, evolution changes from a biological process to an irresistible force of destiny and is imbued with value regardless of the outcomes it produces.

Though ostensibly disagreeing with Levine, Myers accepts Levine's worldview. In doing so, Myers defines the value of endangered species in terms of what they will contribute to the evolutionary process and to future rates of speciation. Once again, without anyone noticing, evolution moves from the status of biological process to a reason for being. Present species, endangered or otherwise, become the sacrifices offered to satisfy this biological deity. Perhaps not completely comfortable with this rationale, Myers resorts to human utilitarianism as a second reason for saving endangered species. His own example says, in effect, "save the golden tamarin because it may one day provide a cure for cancer (or AIDS or sterility or the common cold)." But if this argument was ever taken seriously, it could have only one outcome: the capture and domestication of the tamarins, and species like them, born and bred to die infected with human diseases. The authentic value of the creature itself is not only never defined, it is never addressed. No one even perceives its existence.

The tragedy of Myers's argument to value species based on economic and anthropocentric incentive is vividly portrayed in the travesty of so-called sea turtle ranching, which is considered a form of "commercial conservation." One species of sea turtle, the green turtle, is its main object. "Surplus" green turtle eggs are gathered and hatched in captivity, and the turtles are raised to market size and sold. Supposedly this will reduce the demand for wild turtles and thus save future populations.[8]

David Ehrenfeld, former editor of the journal *Conservation Biology,* comments on both the greed and stupidity of this approach. In a perceptive essay entitled "The Business of Conservation," Ehrenfeld points out that aside from the myriad and difficult problems of keeping and raising the turtles in captivity, such an approach actually increases the world demand for sea turtle products. Such demand inevitably not only makes greater demands on wild turtle populations through legitimate egg collection but also makes it extremely attractive to poach wild turtles. And poaching will always be cheaper than ranching.[9] The high-class consumers who desire such products, no matter how sophisticated they consider their tastes, won't be able to tell the difference. Ehrenfeld summarizes his case succinctly: "The power of global demand erodes all safeguards. . . . Thus the commercial ranching of green turtles inevitably brings us around again on the downward spiral—a little closer to the extinction of the remaining populations. By no stretch of the imagination is this conservation."[10]

Such is the fate of every so-called value system or ethical philosophy that makes human need or want the measure of every creature's worth. This is where Myers's value system for saving endangered species ultimately ends.

We would be unfair to expect the short exchange of opinion between Myers and Levine to provide an extended treatment of a complex ethical issue. But it is most discouraging that neither Levine nor Myers addresses the most significant question: What is the value of living things? A question of great philosophical and ethical importance is ignored simply through redefinition of the argument.

Such a debate reflects the utter moral barrenness and intellectual poverty of the secular ethic. But all who value the search for real truth should see in the shallowness of this exchange more reason than ever to be grateful for the Word of God. The covenant of Genesis 9 squarely faces the value of created things, and places them just as squarely under God's direct provision and protection. "I now establish my covenant with you . . . and with every living creature that was with you—the birds, the livestock, and all the wild animals, all those that came out of the ark with you—every living creature on earth. . . . Never again will all life be cut off by the waters of a flood" (Genesis 9:9-11).

What is the fate of those who set out by design, by ignorance or by selfishness to destroy what God has pledged himself to protect? What will be the outcome of having been on the wrong side of God on an issue of covenant preservation, the fate of the world's endangered species? It is on the basis of God's covenant protection of his creation, consistent with the value he has already imparted to it and with his determination to redeem it, that we believe it matters very much.

The Covenant Continued

God's covenant relations with human and nonhuman creation did not cease with the Noachian covenant. Succeeding covenants between God and his people included the Abrahamic (Genesis 15:1-21; 17:6-8), Mosaic (Exodus 19—24) and Davidic (2 Samuel 7:5-16; Psalm 89) covenants. In each, God sovereignly administers their benefits by grace, just as he did with Noah. The relationship between God and his people is well expressed in the words of Exodus. "I will take you as my own people, and I will be your God. Then you will know that I am the LORD" (Exodus 6:7).

Though God's covenant is a covenant of grace, it does not imply that humanity, as God's image on earth, can do as it pleases. Just as the Lord "is the faithful God, keeping his covenant of love to a thousand generations" (Deuteronomy 7:9). He also states the promise that "If you pay attention to these laws and are careful to follow them, then the LORD your God will keep his covenant of love with you" (Deuteronomy 7:12). The Mosaic covenant began with the Ten Commandments but went on to amplify their principles in every sphere of personal, social, political and religious activity. The spiritual reality of the covenant was one which God intended his people to express in every area of daily life.

An example of the practical implications of such a covenant relationship with creation is given in Leviticus 25. Here God prescribes

powerful measures to teach his people a right attitude toward the land
he gave them. He was concerned with curbing human greed as well as
with nurturing the land itself. For this reason, he commanded the
Israelites to observe a "land sabbath."

> When you enter the land I am going to give you, the land itself must
> observe a sabbath to the LORD. For six years sow your fields, and for
> six years prune your vineyards and gather their crops. But in the
> seventh year the land is to have a sabbath of rest, a sabbath to the
> LORD. Do not sow your fields or prune your vineyards. Do not reap
> what grows of itself or harvest the grapes of your untended vines.
> The land is to have a year of rest. Whatever the land yields during
> the sabbath year will be food for you—for yourself, your manservant
> and maidservant, and the hired worker and temporary resident who
> live among you, as well as for your livestock and the wild animals in
> your land. Whatever the land produces may be eaten. (Leviticus
> 25:2-7)

God was concerned not only with people but also with the land he had
given his people as an inheritance. His concern remains. If we present
the gospel only as a sequence of creation, fall and Christ, we give the
impression that Genesis 3 through Matthew 1 is a kind of grand
parenthesis, and that Christ could have been Eve's son as well as Mary's.
This is a great mistake. God was not ashamed to give his people a land
"flowing with milk and honey," not only to meet their needs but also
to provide a witness of the whole created order of what life with God
was intended to be like.

The Israelites' prosperity was not to come from treating the land like
a commodity but from tending the land on loan from God. It was God's
intention that by careful observance of such laws, the land would be
nurtured throughout every succeeding generation and that Israel
would present to a fallen world the model of a redeemed creation.
Because Israel had this responsibility, relation to the land was a religious issue. It was appropriate to treat land abuse as sin (that is, criminal
activity against God), and the God-given right to live in the land could
be revoked.

God made repeated warnings to his people against land abuse
through his prophets, always with the two-edged blade of blessing and
punishment: "But as for you, you are to keep My statutes and My

judgments, and shall not do any of these abominations . . . so that the land may not spew you out" (Leviticus 18:26, 28 NASB).

It is only in taking such a covenant seriously that Christians will demonstrate any depth and meaning to the truth that God sustains the world and our life in it. Tragically, the Israelites never obeyed God's laws regarding the care of the land. Perhaps, like us, they found them too impractical to be obeyed in the real world. But God's laws cannot be ignored indefinitely. Second Chronicles 36 closes the book on the kingdom of Judah with these words:

> He [Nebuchadnezzar] carried into exile to Babylon the remnant, who escaped from the sword, and they became servants to him and to his sons until the kingdom of Persia came to power. The land enjoyed its sabbath rests; all the time of its desolation it rested, until the seventy years were completed in fulfillment of the word of the LORD spoken by Jeremiah. (vv. 20-21)

The tragedy of exile came upon Israel for many reasons, but it is noteworthy that the only reason given in this passage was for Israel's abuse of the land. So the people were taken away "until the land had enjoyed its sabbaths."

The Need for Redemption

On May 10, 1986, Father Josim Morais Tavares, a Catholic priest working in rural Brazil, was assassinated by a hired gunman. Father Tavares was regional coordinator of the Catholic Church's Pastoral Land Commission, an organization designed for the support of rural peasant organizations. He had received many death threats and had survived an attempt on his life in April of the same year. After that attempt Father Tavares had commented, "In spite of everything I want to continue the struggle, trying to bring together the need for peace and the Christian mission of creating a fraternal and just world. . . . May my faith be penetrated by political clarity and impregnated by that courage which is a resurrection of Jesus of Nazareth, the Christ."[11]

Father Tavares's death was not considered important or unusual enough to make the evening news in North America. But it is a testimony to the evil of our world because it was directed against both people and creation. "You want something but don't get it," wrote James. "You kill and covet, but you cannot have what you want" (James

4:2). Everywhere human greed seizes land and oppresses people, stopping at nothing to obtain its desire. God's Word remains current because human beings remain the same, desperately in need of redemption. Isaiah wrote:

> Woe to you who add house to house
>> and join field to field
> till no space is left
>> and you live alone in the land.
> The LORD Almighty has declared in my hearing:
> "Surely the great houses will become desolate,
>> the fine mansions left without occupants." (5:8-9)

The reality of our lives is such that we all fail God repeatedly. If our sin affected us only as individuals, it would be of serious consequence. But it has a much greater effect. Our evil separates us not only from God but also from the world around us. Moral conduct has ecological implications.

> Hear the word of the LORD, you Israelites,
>> because the LORD has a charge to bring
>> against you who live in the land:
> "There is no faithfulness, no love,
>> no acknowledgment of God in the land.
> There is only cursing, lying and murder,
>> stealing and adultery;
> they break all bounds,
>> and bloodshed follows bloodshed.
> Because of this the land mourns,
>> and all who live in it waste away;
> the beasts of the field and the birds of the air
>> and the fish of the sea are dying. (Hosea 4:1-3)

Expressions like "no faithfulness, no love, no acknowledgment of God in the land" certainly describe the kind of covenant breaking practiced in modern culture. Modern people find it hard to believe that moral evil brings, among other things, ecological devastation. Yet that is God's word to us, both then and today.

The desire to "save the world" from environmental disaster without facing the moral and physical consequences of our own evil is characteristic of the modern environmental movement, and of the philosophies, like New Age, which sustain it. An excellent example of this kind of thinking is found in the works of philosopher Thomas Berry, author of *The Dream of the Earth*. Berry warns his readers that the Bible is the wrong place to look for a "theology of nature." He believes that a global age of environmental consciousness is now upon us, an age that requires us to develop a new story of the universe. The story Berry believes is that the cosmos itself is the teacher, that its destiny is our destiny and its values our values as the consciousness of the earth.[12]

Berry, with many other environmental philosophers, regards the cosmos itself and its evolution as God's primary word to humanity and asserts that we must derive our moral standards from it. But the tragic failure of such systems of thought is that they can neither take into account nor give explanation for the reality of evil and the desire in each of us to escape it. As Kenneth Woodward of *Newsweek* observed after conversing with Berry and reviewing his ideas, "The human species has no doubt sinned against the environment, but it has also sinned against itself—and God—which is why stories of redemption still possess power, even in an ecological age."[13] It is to that story that we now turn.

Redemption

The reality of evil in ourselves and in our world forces us to the reality of redemption—at least, to the reality of wanting to be redeemed. Being hungry does not mean that you will get bread. But it would be odd for someone to be hungry who had no stomach. Being oppressed by evil, within and without, does not mean that you will be freed from it. But if slavery to evil is our intended state, it is very odd that we should always be hoping for and expecting something better.

The concept of redemption is, like covenant, not always well understood in the present age. Simply put, redemption is the deliverance from some evil by payment of a price, or ransom. Redemption is not an idea separate from covenant but inherent in it. The covenant of the sabbath was also meant to be the beginning of redemption.

> Then have the trumpet sounded everywhere on the tenth day of the seventh month; on the Day of Atonement sound the trumpet throughout your land. Consecrate the fiftieth year and proclaim a liberty throughout the land to all its inhabitants. It shall be a jubilee for you. (Leviticus 25:9-10)

This jubilee was to be celebrated every fiftieth year, the year after the seventh sabbath. It was in this "sabbath of sabbaths" that all slaves were to be freed, and all property acquired within the last fifty years returned to its original owners. No crops were sown, no harvests gathered. God promised that his provision in the years preceding the jubilee would be so great that none would be needed. Humanity and creation would rejoice together as one in this great celebration. The curse of Adam had been to eat bread by the sweat of his face. The joy of jubilee was to know God's freedom from this relentless toil. The curse of Eden would begin to work backward.

Because the Israelites lacked both faith and obedience (which are not, as some suppose, opposites but complements) they never fully enjoyed the jubilee that God intended. Their decision to abandon faith in God for self-reliance was an exchange of freedom for toil, and of abundance for want. Today self-reliance is promoted by the same appeals to human pride, and receives the same reward.

Such bondage is self-imposed, yet God speaks with compassion to people living in their own chosen slavery. As before, he speaks of a covenant, but now he speaks of a covenant of redemption.

> In that day I will make a covenant for them
>> with the beasts of the field and the birds of the air
>> and the creatures that move along the ground.
> Bow and sword and battle
>> I will abolish from the land,
>> so that all may lie down in safety.
> I will betroth you to me forever;
>> I will betroth you in righteousness and justice,
>> in love and compassion.
> I will betroth you in faithfulness,
>> and you will acknowledge the LORD.
>
> "In that day that I will respond,"
>> declares the LORD—
> "I will respond to the skies,
>> and they will respond to the earth;
> and the earth will respond to the grain,
>> the new wine and oil,

and they will respond to Jezreel." (Hosea 2:18-22)

Jezreel is a real place in Israel, but it is also a Hebrew word meaning "God plants." In knowing that meaning, we understand the beauty of the message that follows.

> I will plant her for myself in the land;
>> I will show my love to the one I called "Not my loved one."
> I will say to those called "Not my people," "You are My people";
>> and they will say, "You are my God!" (Hosea 2:23)

When God sows a new land, and himself in it, he promises that the land will respond both to him and to us, and we will respond as well. Creation will live out the order of life that it was always meant to have, and we will be a part of it. So when the psalmist and the prophets speak of mountains bowing down and trees clapping their hands, they are not indulging in some sort of primitive, simple-minded musing. They are using human behavioral actions (bowing and clapping) to describe how the very nature of creation will be changed so that it can respond to God and to us in ways that are impossible for it now.

But how can these things take place, short of destroying the present creation and making a new one, and us with it? It is to this question that redemption speaks, and its voice again rises out of covenant.

> "The time is coming," declares the LORD,
>> "when I will make a new covenant
> with the house of Israel
>> and with the house of Judah. . . .
> I will put my laws in their minds
>> and write it on their hearts.
> I will be their God,
>> and they will be my people.
> No longer will a man teach his neighbor,
>> or a man his brother, saying 'Know the LORD,'
> because they will all know me,
>> from the least of them to the greatest. . . .
>
> "For I will forgive their wickedness
>> and will remember their sins no more." (Jeremiah 31:31-34)

Yet this new covenant is not so much a covenant with new kinds of rules as it is a covenant for new kinds of people. For this kind of covenant to work, a radical change in human nature is demanded, as well as a radical change in creation.

By itself, knowing this isn't likely to make one feel any better. It only serves to deepen our despair. Over a generation ago Aldo Leopold understood very well the need for a genuine conversion of the human heart if there was ever to be a hope for better treatment of the land. "No important change in ethics," he wrote, "was ever accomplished without an internal change in our intellectual emphasis, loyalties, affections, and convictions."[14]

Near the end of his life, Leopold realized bitterly that attempts to establish a genuine environmental ethic without such a change in human nature were futile. "In our attempt to make conservation easy we have made it trivial," he wrote. "When the logic of history hungers for bread and we hand out a stone, we are at pains to explain how much the stone resembles bread."[15]

We must understand the logic of God's covenant before we can begin to make any sense of the logic of history. We must choose to become partners in that covenant before we can expect to make more than trivial efforts at conservation.

The Covenant of Christ

Unlike the covenant with Noah, which could not be broken, God's other covenants continue to be broken by human disobedience. Humans continue to be dominated and controlled by evil, in themselves and toward creation. The outcome is death for both. Without redemption, slavery to evil would continue, and so would an endless cycle of death and judgment.

In all these things, we are made painfully aware that we share with creation both the need and the hope of a redeemer. For by ourselves, we have no hope of attaining either a new nature or a new creation.

The change in human nature has been begun by an act of God. The covenants which came before were shadows of a substance accomplished when God not only identified himself with creation and humanity but became part of both in the person of Jesus Christ. By his death and resurrection, Christ removed the penalty of human sin, which is death, for us and for creation. His death was a payment the human race did not have the funds to make, both for our disobedience to God and for the harm which that disobedience brought to creation. Redemption demands a price, and the Bible describes that price as "redemption through his [Christ's] blood" (Ephesians 1:7) and that "Christ redeemed us . . . by becoming a curse for us" (Galatians 3:13).

His resurrection from that death was the beginning of the power of a new life in the world. When persons place their trust in Christ to be forgiven for the evil they have done, and to live under his authority as their God, the story of redemption begins. The meaning of God's promise to write new laws on our hearts and minds becomes clear. The agent of this transformation is the person of God in the Holy Spirit. By this act of God, humans are rescued from the futility of trying to be nice people to the reality of beginning to become new creatures—the initiation of a new covenant relationship with God, a God they can now call "Father."

The Bible itself describes this covenant of (and with) Jesus Christ as the consummation of the ages (Galatians 4:4) and everlasting in scope (Hebrews 13:20). The benefits of such a covenant, to those who enter it, include the power of the Holy Spirit to live in obedience to God, the freedom from being controlled by evil, and to begin to become, in nature and character, like Christ himself.

We said that the story of redemption begins here, in individual lives. That is not where it ends. It has been common within the Christian community to focus on the God-human aspect of this covenant and ignore its implications for the rest of creation. This is because many passages that describe this covenant have an emphasis on God and humanity (which is understandable, since the Bible was written to be read and understood by humans, not sea otters or spotted owls) and because theologians have encouraged this emphasis to the point of ignoring all others. Karl Barth, one of the most influential Reformed theologians of the twentieth century, flatly stated that creation was not involved in this redemption. "The purpose and therefore the meaning of creation," he wrote, "is to make possible the history of God's covenant with man, which has its beginning, its center and its culmination in Jesus Christ."[16]

The idea that creation is merely the stage and props in which the drama of God's covenant and redemption can be played out in history is not a biblical one. That Barth's view was deficient in this respect has been noted by other theologians, as well as by the witness of Scripture. The eminent Old Testament scholar Gerhard von Rad observed, "The greater part of what we call the Old Testament has to say about what we call nature has simply never been considered. If I am right, we are nowadays in serious danger of looking at the theological problem of the Old Testament far too much from the one-sided standpoint of an historical conditioned philosophy."[17]

The place of creation in redemption is a prominent feature of both the Old and New Testaments. The needs and hopes of creation for a redeemer we have already seen, for this is a common theme in Old Testament prophecy. The fulfillment of that hope for creation is addressed in the New Testament.

Christ's death and resurrection have not only personal consequences for me but also cosmic consequences for creation. God's saving grace through Christ not only pays the price for people but redeems an oppressed cosmos. This does not demean the work of Christ, but rather amplifies it. Just as the sin of Adam affected all creation, so the sacrifice of Christ begins the redemption of it.

Such consequences are always clearly understood throughout the New Testament. The reconciliation with God achieved through the life, death and resurrection of Christ extends to all creation. This was clearly Paul's understanding when he wrote,

> He [Christ] is the image of the invisible God, the firstborn over all creation. For by him *all things* were created: things in heaven and on earth, visible and invisible; . . . all things were created by him and for him. . . . For God was pleased to have all his fullness dwell in him, and through him to reconcile to himself *all things* . . . by making peace through his blood, shed on the cross. (Colossians 1:15-16, 19-20)

Clearly the "all things" referred to in this context are the same "all things" that Christ created—the entire physical universe. Many other New Testament passages underscore Christ's defeat of all rebellious powers and the resulting restoration of God's purpose and intended order in all creation (Romans 8:19; 2 Corinthians 5:19).

This message of cosmic redemption is not confined to the New

Testament. Recall that the covenant established following the flood was not merely with Noah but "between me and the earth" and "every living creature" (Genesis 9:12-13). The redemptive promises set forth in Isaiah are filled with images of all creation participating in the saving and restoring work of God. "No longer will they call you Deserted, or name your land Desolate. But you will be called Hephzibah [my delight is in her], and your land Beulah [married]" (Isaiah 62:4).

When I was a child, I often sang a favorite song:

I have a song I love to sing, since I have been redeemed,

Of my Redeemer, Savior, King, since I have been redeemed.

I can remember singing it even before I knew what the words meant. But after I understood the refrain, it came to be a song of celebration. What made this a wonderful message was that it was personal, directed to me as an individual.

Redemption is certainly personal, but it is never merely personal. Sometimes we personalize this message to the point of forgetting everyone and everything around us. It is just *because* I have been redeemed that I may not—indeed must not—ignore the broader implications of that redemption. To know that all creation shares in being the object of this redemptive work does not diminish my love for Christ or my joy in being redeemed. Rather, it reveals to me a Savior who is truly worthy of my trust, worship and devotion, for his act of redemption is so powerful that it not only saves me but changes the nature of the physical universe forever.

Dietrich Bonhoeffer seems to have grasped this mystery, this linkage between our redemption and creation's, when he wrote,

What a strange paradise is this hill of Golgotha, this Cross, this blood, this broken body. What a strange tree of life, this tree on which God must suffer and die—but it is in fact the kingdom of God and the resurrection.... The tree of life, the Cross of Christ, [in] the middle of the fallen and preserved world of God, for us that is the end of the story of paradise.[18]

Redemption does not merely look back to a triumphant resurrection or merely gaze ahead to a glorious future. The reality of redemption gives us reason and power to celebrate the freedom we have in the present. Life is not a meaningless bore or a bad joke. Because we have been "bought with a price," we should glorify God with our lives (1 Corinthians 6:20). As God's children, we have a special responsibility toward the rest of creation (Romans 8:18-22). Indeed, the Bible declares that all creation eagerly awaits the revealing of the children of God (Romans 8:19). Because we live in covenant bond with God, we begin the process of restoring creation. The completion of this work is an act of God, and we cannot presume to do that. But we do, we must, demonstrate the reality of Christ's work in our treatment of creation, and we should expect substantial healing to occur if we treat creation in obedience to the covenant God established with it. If we do, we will begin to understand the meaning of the Amish proverb that says, "We did not inherit the land from our fathers. We are borrowing it from our children."

Questions for Thought and Discussion

1. Who are the parties of the covenant described in Genesis 9? What are the terms of this covenant? What evidence is presented that this covenant is not exclusively between God and humans?

2. In the Bible, what is the rainbow consistently used as a symbol of? Why is this an appropriate and forceful symbol for the Genesis 9 covenant?

3. In what ways are humanity and creation linked in the Bible's view of covenant and redemption?

4. What are the implications of the Genesis 9 covenant today? Why does the knowledge that creation will be redeemed with us matter in the way we treat creation today?

6

Ruling & Subduing
The Uniqueness of Being Human

*Be fruitful and increase in number; fill the
earth and subdue it. Rule over the fish of the
sea and the birds of the air and over every
living creature that moves on the ground.*
GENESIS 1:28

W HAT DO YOU THINK OF WHEN YOU THINK OF A "RULER"? WHAT
do you imagine when you hear the word *subdue?* Perhaps
you think of pomp and power, force and fear, cunning and
coercion. These are the traits we most often see in rulers and in those
who subdue others. When Lynn White Jr. wrote in his famous essay that
Christianity insisted that "it is God's will that man exploit nature for his
proper ends,"[1] or when Aldo Leopold claimed that a new land ethic
would change "the role of *Homo sapiens* from conqueror of the land
community to plain member and citizen of it,"[2] it was Genesis 1:28 they
were attempting to repudiate.

If we were to compile a list of rulers and subduers, it would not be
the same as a list of saints and servants. The tragic history of our race
is a story of millions of wicked people trying to "rule and subdue" (or
rather, exploit and subjugate) one another. The names of the more
successful ones, Genghis Khan, Nebuchadnezzar, Julius Caesar, Herod
the Great, Atilla the Hun, Stalin, Mao Zedong, Hitler and Idi Amin,
cast a grim shadow on the mind and drench the pages of history in the
blood of the innocent. It is understandable that the world should
associate the content of Genesis 1:28 with these sorts of images. But

every word has two dimensions of meaning: (1) its definition, the actual objective content of the ideas expressed, and (2) its connotation, the association it acquires in its use in the world. The two are not always the same, and mistaking one for the other can mislead us.

To understand what God's Word means to us, we should begin by trying to understand what it meant to Adam and Eve, to whom it was originally spoken, and to see how they responded to it. Adam and Eve were not (originally) like us. They had no knowledge of good and evil. They were sinless, innocent and unfallen. They had no knowledge of the long human bloodbath in our history. What did ruling and subduing mean to them? More importantly, what did it mean to God? We should begin to answer these questions by examining their biblical setting.

Subduing the Earth

Take the case of subduing first. We can begin to discover its meaning by eliminating some of the things it probably did not mean to Adam. It is unlikely that God's instruction to subdue the earth meant "kill and eat all the animals." God's instructions to Adam are, "I give you every seed-bearing plant on the face of the whole earth and every tree that has fruit with seed in it. They will be yours for food" (Genesis 1:29). With these instructions, Adam probably would not have looked at an ostrich as a large pair of drumsticks or a hippopotamus as a ton of chuck steak. Neither did Adam require the skins and furs of animals to cover himself, for "the man and his wife were both naked, and they felt no shame" (Genesis 2:25). It also seems unlikely that God's command to subdue the earth meant to mine and exploit its inorganic matter.

Modern technology, as we know it today, developed from two basic human needs. One was to control the immediate environment, more specifically to keep warm. The other was to increase food production. These uses had no application in Adam's world. To this day the native peoples of tropical climates, where food is abundant and physical surroundings warm, have developed little technology and wear little clothing. Why should they? What possible use could it serve? The man and his wife were not only not ashamed to be naked; they also were not uncomfortable. *Subduing,* in this context, cannot even mean "start

some high-intensity agriculture."While there is instruction to "cultivate
and keep" Eden (Genesis 2:15), it seems a pleasant enough task in a
land where "the LORD God made all kinds of trees to grow out of the
ground—trees that were pleasing to the eye and good for food"
(Genesis 2:9).

Taken together, these alternatives cover the typical spectrum of
exploitative acts that most people associate with the phrase "rule and
subdue." In Adam's world those acts are inappropriate. Indeed, they
would be acts without purpose or meaning. In this context, the term
subdue is apparently God's instruction to Adam to continue to bring
what God has created into conformity with his ways and purposes. In
a world without sin, we are not unkind to Adam to point out that this
would have been neither a difficult nor an unpleasant task.

Certainly, Adam's first act of subduing (and perhaps, tragically, his
last) was to name the animals. Here we see Adam cooperating with God
in continuing to order what God had made. It was God who brought
order out of chaos. But now, not out of need but out of love, he involves
a human being in the continuing work of the ordering of creation. In
the mind of God, this was what it meant to subdue.

Ruling over Creation

Many persons find the idea of "ruling over" creation even more difficult
to accept than subduing it. How can the idea of man as ruler and
creation as his subject lead to anything but creation's destruction? For
our race, it is hard to find examples of truly good rulers, though
perhaps there have been a few. But before we embrace the negative
conclusion about what "ruling" might mean, we ought to examine what
God might mean, rather than what we assume.

God himself is a ruler, and is not ashamed to describe himself to us
in those terms. At times he has shared with us his mind and heart on
the subject of ruling. Long before his people, the Israelites, had
thought of having a king, God gave them prophetic instruction about
the kingship which, if followed, would have marked their king as
distinctive among all the rulers of the earth.

The king, moreover, must not acquire great numbers of horses for
himself or make the people return to Egypt to get more of them,
for the LORD has told you, "You are not to go back that way again."

He must not take many wives, or his heart will be led astray. He must not accumulate large amounts of silver and gold.

When he takes the throne of his kingdom, he is to write for himself on a scroll a copy of this law, taken from that of the priests, who are Levites. It is to be with him, and he is to read it all the days of his life, so that he may learn to revere the LORD his God and follow carefully all the words of this law and these decrees and not consider himself better than his brothers and turn from the law to the right or to the left. Then he and his descendants will reign a long time over his kingdom in Israel." (Deuteronomy 17:16-20)

Ironically, it was Solomon, a man who could and should have been Israel's greatest king, who brought ruin to himself by his failure to observe these instructions. He collected seven hundred wives and three hundred concubines, and

Solomon accumulated chariots and horses; he had fourteen hundred chariots and twelve thousand horses. . . . The king made silver as common in Jerusalem as stones. . . . [His] horses were imported from Egypt and from Kue. . . . King Solomon . . . loved many foreign women besides Pharaoh's daughter—Moabites, Ammonites, Edomites, Sidonians and Hittites. . . . As Solomon grew old, his wives turned his heart after other gods. . . . He followed Ashtoreth the goddess of the Sidonians, and Molech the detestable god of the Ammonites. So Solomon did evil in the eyes of the LORD. (1 Kings 10:26-30; 11:1, 4-6)

The Words and Deeds of God

If God measures human kings differently from the way we do, he judges himself by an even stricter standard. For God is a ruler, the greatest ruler of the universe, monarch of galaxies and sovereign of solar systems. But how does God rule his own people? God's greatest promise to Israel was that one day he would rule them himself, without the intermediary of prophet, priest or king.

"For to us a child is born," wrote Isaiah, "to us a son is given, and the government will be on his shoulders. And he will be called Wonderful Counselor, Mighty God, Everlasting Father, Prince of Peace. Of the increase of his government and peace there will be no end. He will reign on David's throne and over his kingdom" (9:6-7). Today we know that prophecy for what it is, a description of Jesus Christ, the Messiah, the Son of God, the greatest and most powerful ruler that the universe and all its history will ever know. But how does Jesus rule? By word and deed, Jesus' idea of ruling proves very different from the world's. Jesus said,

> You know that the rulers of the Gentiles lord it over them, and their high officials exercise authority over them. Not so with you. Instead, whoever wants to become great among you must be your servant, and whoever wants to be first must be your slave—just as the Son of Man did not come to be served, but to serve, and to give his life as a ransom for many. (Matthew 20:25-28)

In the life of Jesus, these words proved to be no empty rhetoric. They were portrayed in a powerful object lesson on the eve of his death.

> Jesus knew that the Father had put all things under his power, and that he had come from God and was returning to God; so he got up from the meal, took off his outer clothing, and wrapped a towel around his waist. After that, he poured water into a basin and began to wash his disciples' feet, drying them with the towel that was wrapped around him. . . .
>
> When he had finished washing their feet, he put on his clothes and returned to his place. "Do you understand what I have done for you?" he asked them. "You call me 'Teacher' and 'Lord,' and rightly so, for that is what I am. Now that I, your Lord and Teacher, have washed your feet, you also should wash one another's feet. I have set you an example that you should do as I have done for you." (John 13:3-5, 12-15)

In the eyes of God, the one who rules is the one who serves. So humans are called to rule and subdue the creation by serving it. In fact, the Hebrew phrase of Genesis 2:15, normally translated "till and keep," could be as accurately rendered "serve and preserve."

In ruling the universe, God has not turned the cosmos into a police state where every unbeliever is taken into a concentration camp to be tortured into accepting his claims. A day will come when God's claims are established. For the present, God rules with patience, gentleness and mercy, and "causes his sun to rise on the evil and the good" (Matthew 5:45) by restraining some of human depravity by the authority of government, and by providing for the needs of all life everywhere.

"You open your hand," wrote the psalmist, "and satisfy the desires of every living thing" (Psalm 145:16).

God demonstrates his love and mercy toward humans even when they fail to acknowledge him. God has never asked of any person more than he could give, and God has given all he has to us, even his own life. He tells his servants to pray for people who don't believe and to bless the persecutors who harm them. His loving kindness toward each of us, in a thousand secret ways that only God and (perhaps) we know, is everlasting. In the same way, God rules creation.

> He covers the sky with clouds;
>> he supplies the earth with rain
>> and makes grass grow on the hills.
> He provides food for the cattle
>> and for the young ravens when they call. (Psalm 147:8-9)
> These all look to you
>> to give them their food at the proper time.
> When you give it to them,
>> they gather it up;
> when you open your hand,
>> they are satisfied with good things.
> When you hide your face,
>> they are terrified;
> When you take away their breath,
>> they die and return to the dust.
> When you send your Spirit,
>> they are created,
>> and you renew the face of the earth. (Psalm 104:27-30)

Jack Cottrell writes, "There seems to be a relationship of real intimacy between the Creator and his creation. We get the impression that God loves the world of nature and cares for it with a tenderness and concern that we might expect in a gardener caring for his prize roses."[3] Cottrell is close to the mark. God describes the land he has chosen for his own people, Israel, in this way:

> The land you are entering to take over is not like the land of Egypt, from which you have come, where you planted your seed and irrigated it by foot as in a vegetable garden. But the land you are crossing the Jordan to take possession of is a land of mountains and

valleys that drinks rain from heaven. It is a land the LORD your God cares for; the eyes of the LORD your God are continually on it, from the beginning of the year to its end. (Deuteronomy 11:10-12)

God rules his creation with love and care, providing for its needs in both general and specific ways. He rules with an intimacy of knowledge which surpasses our wildest imaginings. "Are not two sparrows sold for a penny?" said Jesus. "Yet not one of them will fall to the ground apart from the will of your Father" (Matthew 10:29). Does this mean that God attends the funerals of sparrows? Apparently, according to Jesus, it is so.

The Image of God

Humans alone, among all created things, are said to be made in the image of God. This does not, of course, mean that we physically look like God (and when we look in the mirror in the morning we can be glad of that). To understand what it does mean, we need to understand what the term *image* has historically meant to the people to whom this story was originally told.

Most ancient peoples believed in a multitude of gods. These were often worshiped as images representing the gods' forms and attributes. But the intelligent image worshiper did not believe that the image was the god itself. Rather, as a representation of the god, the image provided a focus for the god to express itself, to exert its power and manifest its presence. Jehovah was unique among the ancient gods in that he forbade the use of images in his worship. This is expressed in the second commandment: "You shall not make for yourself an idol [i.e. a graven image] in the form of anything in heaven above or on the earth beneath or in the waters below" (Exodus 20:4).

This commandment was not merely the prohibition of the worship of false gods, but a prohibition against the worship of the true God, as well as all false ones, through images. For no image of God can be found in all creation, save one, and that has been graven by God himself. "Let us make man in our image, in our likeness." And understanding this, we can see the sense of what follows: "Let them rule over the fish of the sea and the birds of the air, over the livestock, over all the earth, and over all the creatures that move along the ground" (Genesis 1:26). What else would, or could, the image of God do?

As we share with all creation the blessing to be fruitful and multiply, so, as the image of God, we receive a unique charge. After bidding humans, as he had to the other creatures of creation, to "be fruitful and increase in number," God adds, "Fill the earth and subdue it. Rule over the fish of the sea and the birds of the air and over every living creature that moves on the ground" (Genesis 1:28).

After Adam and Eve are given the command to rule and subdue, they are given three specific tasks in Eden. The first two are to cultivate and keep the garden. The third, given later, is to name the animals.

Cultivating certainly implies some change, growth and development. But it is growth and change of a positive, constructive nature, as when we speak of "cultivating" a friendship. It means to assist something to achieve its own natural and highest tendencies. The Hebrew understanding of this concept was stronger. The word translated "cultivate" (*'ābad*) comes from the Hebrew word meaning "to serve" or, more literally, "to be a slave to." In an agrarian society, it was natural to think of cultivation in this way. How else would one "serve" the ground?

And we all know what "keeping" means. It means to preserve, protect and maintain. The fact that both are here used to describe Adam's care of the same object, Eden, can only mean that neither God nor Adam viewed them as conflicting goals. To subdue Eden apparently meant to retain the goodness and beauty which God gave it, while actively serving Eden through managing (cultivating) it to better enhance and manifest the qualities hidden within it. The Hebrew word *šāmar*, translated as "keep" in English, is the same word used in the familiar benediction of Numbers 6:22-26. Moses is instructed to tell Aaron and his sons to bless the Israelites with these words, "The LORD bless you and *keep [šāmar]* you; the LORD make his face shine upon you and be gracious to you; the LORD turn his face toward you and give you peace." Clearly humankind is instructed to "keep" the garden as the Lord "keeps" us.

Naming implies knowing, an intimate and particular knowledge of what something is. To most people, sparrows are only little brown birds. But any good ornithologist knows at least a dozen differences between swamp sparrows, chipping sparrows, field sparrows, fox sparrows, song sparrows, vesper sparrows, lark sparrows and all the rest. So naming implies this sort of knowledge and a (rightful) exercise of authority by

Adam. Naming also implies identity and value, just as our individual names signify. Collectively, in these three actions—cultivating, keeping and naming—we have a glimpse, albeit brief, of how an unfallen man went about subduing an equally unfallen world.

The Alternatives
In these few words of Scripture we can begin to understand what God had in mind when he called us to "rule and subdue" the earth. Not a statement of primitive Hebrew arrogance now armed, as Lynn White Jr. supposed, with the power of twentieth-century technology, but a call to accept our rightful place in creation as its servant and protector. In that place we bear the image of our Lord, becoming, as idol worshipers had vainly hoped for images of stone and wood, a focus and channel for God's activity on earth. Clearly the command to rule and subdue, given both the context of Eden and the example of God's rule toward us, cannot mean "exercise despotic authority over nature." Rather, it can only mean that human beings, whom God has made great, must be creation's servants. By Christ's example we are instructed to put the welfare of the nonhuman world above our own, to seek its good first, to rule as servants.

To do this successfully requires a right response from us. It requires us to accept our rightful place in creation. We are creatures made from the dust, and we need a healthy creation to survive, even if that is not the most noble reason for saving it. We belong in creation and are a part of it, but we also have a special place in it. And we must, in accepting that place, accept the responsibilities that come with it.

The inconsistencies of most secular environmental ethics are that they demean human management of creation while at the same time demanding such management. So Aldo Leopold, in his classic work *A Sand County Almanac*, is on one page telling us to accept a role as "plain members and citizens" of the natural community, while telling us some pages later that wilderness should be saved because it is "the raw material out of which man has hammered the artifact of civilization"—in other words, because of its value to the human community.[4]

In contrast, the Bible states that we have a special place in creation as rulers and that we have a responsibility to care for it because God entrusted it to us. In a ruling monarchy, however, abdication can result in anarchy if the throne has no heir. So humanity's abdication of rightful, God-given responsibilities toward creation is as harmful as its abuses. The question is not "Will humans rule nature?" We already do (at least in part), whether we like it or not. The real question is "How will we rule?" That is, will our model be an earthly despot or a divine servant? From the perspective of Scripture, we can accept our role as creation's "rulers" with both enthusiasm and humility. With enthusiasm, because we can rejoice with God in the special role he has given us to bear his image on earth. With humility, because we receive this task by God's choice, not our cleverness, and because we will be held accountable to God for our actions toward creation, as well as for our care of it.

The Implications

Practically, there are four aspects we must consider if we would understand a Christian view (and task) of ruling and subduing creation. The first is *knowledge*. If we would begin to rule creation as God does, we must begin to understand what creation is and how creation works. We must not think that meat and milk come from grocery stores. We must not call a warbler a sparrow or a spruce a pine, and we must begin to see the connections between all these things and everything else. We must learn to know creation as Adam began to know it, on a first name, right name, basis. Only in this way can we begin to discover the specific needs of creation and each of its creatures.

But knowledge alone is not enough. The world is full of experts who know about everything and care about nothing. The step that follows knowledge must be *concern*, and in that concern, identity. Just as God chooses to make our concerns his concerns, so we must begin to make creation's concerns our concerns if we would presume to rule in the image of God.

Knowledge and concern lead to *sacrifice*. The real solution to environmental problems cannot come simply from improving our technology. One can always squeeze a turnip a little tighter to draw a little more blood, but that is not the right strategy if you care for the life of the turnip. Creation doesn't need a harder squeeze. It needs a lighter touch. We must develop ways of living which demand more sacrifice for us and less torture for everything else. That is a long story, and its details must be told later, but it begins with this simple idea.

Finally, we must work to *redeem* creation, because that is God's ultimate goal for it. Some Christians have argued that because Jesus may return soon, what happens to creation now doesn't really matter. The apostle Paul would have been unable to grasp this kind of eschatology. He wrote,

> The creation waits in eager expectation for the sons of God to be revealed. For the creation was subjected to frustration, not by its own choice, but by the will of the one who subjected it, in hope that the creation itself will be liberated from its bondage to decay and brought into the glorious freedom of the children of God.
>
> We know that the whole creation has been groaning as in the pains of childbirth right up to the present time. (Romans 8:19-22)

It is precisely the reality and possible imminence of Christ's return that gives our work for creation both meaning and urgency.

The goal and outcome of our work as rulers of creation is to assist it to be "fruitful and multiply," a blessing given not only to humans but to all living things. And now we have filled the world, more than five billion people full. Perhaps that is full enough. But what of the rest of creation?

One May evening I took some students to a small pond in the northern Michigan woods. The sun was setting as we sat down beneath the jack pines that grew to the water's edge in an undergrowth of blueberry and bracken fern. On the slope above us, a few spring peepers had begun to call. At this time of year the male peepers, tiny frogs an inch or two long, sing near the water's edge to draw the females to them. Their song is a loud, shrill, one-note "PREEEEEP." In spring, some can be heard throughout the day, but the greatest choruses form at dusk and continue on into the night.

The longer we sat, the darker it became, and the more peepers began to sing. At the same time they began moving down the hill toward the pond. We could hear them coming closer, not only by their singing but now by the hundreds of tiny rustlings about us as they jumped and crawled over pine needles and bracken fern to reach the water. Closer and closer, louder and louder, more and more until we were surrounded, in the gathering dusk, by a moving sea of peepers, singing and struggling all around. There was just light enough to see them, crawling up a bracken fern to find a singing perch, filling their throats with air like tiny balloons about to burst, and then giving forth, at close range, an ear-splitting "PRRREEEP" that made our heads ring and ended all hope of human conversation. But that did not matter, because now we were immersed in the peepers' lives, not ours. And when the concert ended and the peepers had gone away, we laughed together for the sheer joy and power of life, displayed for a moment in the grand efforts of one tiny creature to be fruitful and multiply.

Sometimes, when life seems cold and dead, I think of the peepers and the education they gave me, a glimpse into a world teeming with life beneath my very feet. Everywhere on earth, life struggles to break forth, to be fruitful and multiply. And everywhere on earth, or so it seems, humans are intent on destroying it. But joy unspeakable waits for those who both know and foster the life of the world in a creation destined for redemption.

The Church

This work of redemption must begin on lands entrusted to each Christian individually, and to us as a church corporately. In homes and on farms, on church grounds and camps, at college campuses and retreat centers, we must begin to live out these principles. The church must be, as Francis Schaeffer put it, a "pilot plant,"[5] demonstrating the work of the ways of God. Unless we show both the commitment and practicality of doing things properly in our own house, it will never be an attractive option for our neighbors. Yet it is precisely our neighbors whom we must influence. The lands we can influence directly are small. It is corporations and governments which must be persuaded by words and deeds. Only in this way can we influence the redemption of creation that lies beyond our control.

Each of these ideas deserves careful thought. And much will be said later in this book about the practical work which such attitudes demand. For now, we must simply remember what it means to rule and subdue. If we would rule as God rules, and subdue as God subdues, then we must change both our thoughts and our tactics. To rule creation means to serve creation. Any other response to nature is no imitation of Christ, no help to creation and no witness to the world.

Questions for Thought and Discussion

1. What does it mean to cultivate, keep and name? How would these activities be properly expressed toward creation in our world today?

2. What kinds of people and actions do you associate with ruling and subduing? What is the difference between the world's connotation of these things and the biblical definitions?

3. What are the proper responsibilities of an "image of God" to creation? Why is it necessary for humans to bear the image of God before acting responsibly toward creation?

4. In what ways does a biblical view of ruling and subduing lead to enthusiasm for those who follow it? In what ways should it lead to humility?

7
God's World Today

IT IS THE LAST DECADE OF THE TWENTIETH CENTURY. OVER THIRTY years ago Rachel Carson's *Silent Spring* announced to the world that the environmental crisis was at hand.[2] In the same year (1962) world population had passed the three billion mark. A global epidemic of pesticide-induced deaths was systematically eliminating many species. There were virtually no environmental laws, there was no Environmental Protection Agency, and smog was considered a problem limited to Los Angeles.

Today, curriculum on the environment and environmental problems is required at all grade levels. Federal and state laws regulate air and water quality, pesticide use and numerous other issues of environmental significance. Millions of acres of legally designated wilderness spread across our states, and expanded national parks provide recreation opportunities and wildlife protection.

While we can point to these successes, many problems today are greater than they were thirty years ago. As Christians and stewards of God's creation, we must not only recognize our role as earthkeepers but also be aware of the state of the ark. As we turn our attention to creation today we are reminded that nearly two thousand years ago the apostle Paul spoke of the groanings of creation as it anxiously awaited the lifting of its bondage to decay (Romans 8:19-22). Let us sharpen our ear now to listen again to creation's voice.

The Human Presence
"God blessed them and said to them, 'Be fruitful and increase in number; fill the earth and subdue it' " (Genesis 1:28). A casual glance shows our success in carrying out the numerical part of this biblical mandate. The human population did not reach one billion until 1800. The second billion was added in only another 130 years (1930), and the third required only another thirty years. By 1987 the human population had reached five billion. Before the end of the twentieth century Rachel Carson's 1962 audience of slightly over three billion people will have doubled.

What are the implications and impact of the human presence on creation? The biblical mandate was to fill the earth. How will we know when it is full? What is the carrying capacity of creation? Is the human presence already too great for the proper stewardship of our sacred trust? What should be the church's response to continued population growth?

These are critical questions. But they are questions the church has only recently considered relevant to its theology and mission. Scripture is silent on matters of population growth and optimal population size. We are not told when creation will be full. We are told to seek wisdom. And Christ's parables give many examples of good stewardship. In this case, some revelation may come from creation itself. When we look at a human-dominated landscape, do we see wholeness, beauty and peace (the image of creation in Psalm 104), or do we see something else? When the human presence is overabundant, what is the result?

Rapid growth is characteristic of most developing countries, setting the stage for potential future land shortages of catastrophic proportions. In 1985 *Population Today* magazine predicted that "by the end of this century, shortage of land will have become a critical constraint for about two thirds of the population of developing countries."[3] Between the years 1980 and 2000 the amount of arable land in such countries is expected to fall from 0.37 hectares per person to only 0.25 hectares per person. And there will be growing disparity between those nations with the fastest-growing populations and those with the best (and most) agricultural land (for example, the United States and Canada).[4] "This," wrote *Population Today*, "combined with poverty and strained third world economies, appears to make the mere question of sufficient land irrelevant."[5] Feeding populations of the future will require a level of international cooperation, trade and foresight very different, and much improved, from what we see today.

Tragically, this comes at a time when much of the world's best agricultural land is being converted to other uses. Between 1967 and 1975 some 2.5 million hectares of prime U.S. cropland were converted to urban and residential use. In Canada, half of all farmland lost to urban expansion has come from the best 5 percent of Canadian farmland. Because of this, a loss of one hundred acres of such land requires a replacement of 240 acres of land in one of Canada's western provinces to achieve the same productivity. Britain and France each lose about 2 percent of their cropland every ten years.[6] The prophet Amos foretold of a time of such great prosperity that the plowman would overtake the reaper (Amos 9:13). But the near future may see Amos's prophecy come true in reversed circumstances, as land shortages force cultivation of marginal land faster than crops from traditional farmland can be harvested.

Urbanization of the developing world is occurring at a pace that prevents any possibility of providing adequate social services like medical care, schools and churches. Between 1950 and 1989 the urban population of Brazil rose from 34 percent to 71 percent of the national population. In 1962, Mexico City had five million people. By 1985, with 17.3 million people, it was the largest city in the world. Such urbanization affects not only city populations, but rural ones as well. Between 1970 and 1982 in sub-Saharan Africa, a massive migration from the countryside to the cities caused tremendous problems. During this period, urban populations grew an average of 6 percent annually. This has led to the formation of concentrated, dominant metropolitan areas that receive disproportionately large shares of government attention and funds.[7]

Today, as the church reaches out to the world, the greatest numbers of missionaries are headed into some of the world's most environmentally damaged countries. The poor suffer disproportionately as creation groans, and missionaries move straight into the eye of the environmental storm. Recognition of this has resulted in a major statement on "ecojustice" addressing global environmental problems by the 1990 general assembly of the Presbyterian Church USA. What should be the role of the missionary? Of the average church attender? As the church struggles to minister to the hungry and care for the sick (Matthew 25), one wonders whether we are treating the symptoms rather than the disease. When starvation and sickness are caused by ecosystem collapse due to overpopulation, one must begin to ask what the church should do. We give money to buy grain for the hungry, but we have often been silent on matters of family planning. Reforesting denuded hills and restoring depleted soil have not been considered ministering to the poor. In reality, this is the only long-range solution. The restoration of creation results in wholeness and the return of self-sufficiency to local people.

The church has been guilty of limiting its attention to the human members of creation and forgetting that our responsibility as stewards extends as servants to the whole garden. This narrow view of theology is changing as the church discovers the full message of Scripture. In the remainder of this chapter we focus on several problems facing creation today that demand our attention.

What We Take Out: Nonrenewable Resources to Supply Human Demand

Have you ever run out of money? As consumers, we are familiar with the need to balance our personal budget. As Christians, we are admonished by Scripture to be wise stewards of our gifts. For most of us, this means our financial resources: our income, our savings and our inheritance. It is obvious that there is a limit to how long one can draw on savings and inheritance before the supply is exhausted. Income is left to provide for long-term needs.

How does this apply to our natural resources? Fossil fuels represent creation's savings account, carbon reserves accumulated over eons of time. Our mineral wealth is a gift from the Creator, an inheritance provided to meet human needs. If used properly, the supply is sufficient for the future. If wasted, the reserves of most minerals will be exhausted in but a few more decades. On the income side, we are also blessed with an abundant supply. Solar energy, wind, running water, forests and other biological resources are either a perpetual source or have a natural rate of renewal.

Unfortunately, we are not treating our global resources with the same wisdom that we apply to our personal wealth. We are suffering from what Garrett Hardin has called "the tragedy of the commons."[8] Because the world's resources belong to no one, they are viewed as common property. But who is responsible for their stewardship? All claim the right to use them, but no one is responsible to preserve them.

Some have argued that a significant part of the problem is capitalism. Growth economics dominates the thinking of most countries. But growth economics does not come to grips with conservation of finite natural resources or other negative factors associated with the abuse of creation. Operating from the principle that continued growth is both good and necessary for a healthy economy, resource use becomes the means to that end. To maximize growth, we also maximize resource use.

The early impact on creation in the Western world which arose from the accumulation of wealth is well documented in the book *Changes in the Land.*[9] Within the few decades following the arrival of European colonists, eastern North America's abundant populations of deer, beaver, turkey, waterfowl and other species were decimated and large tracts of forest destroyed. The sustainable creation that had supported Native American people for millennia had been ravaged to supply the goods for a new system of international commerce.

The great stands of red and white pine which had been abundant in the northern lake states of Michigan, Wisconsin and Minnesota had been removed by the early twentieth century. In Michigan, people who wish to see something of what this great forest might have been like will find it confined to some forty acres within the Hartwick Pines State Park. Not many miles away the ghost town of Deward (named, somewhat corruptly, after past Michigan timber baron David Ward) sits astride a barren landscape of scrub and brush that, after over eighty years, has still not recovered from the logging practiced around this company town in the late nineteenth and early twentieth centuries. Deward is but a single example, repeated throughout the earth, of the legacy of our forebears. It is a powerful example that all economies are ultimately resource-based and that no economy which does not use resources sustainably can itself be sustained.

The Bad Side of the Good Life

The United States consumes a disproportionate share of world resources. For many items, per capita consumption is twice that of most other developed countries. Our national lack of emphasis on conservation and a poor record of recycling (compared to countries like Japan and Sweden) is a significant part of our problem. With 3 percent of world oil reserves, the United States accounts for 30 percent of world consumption. With less than 5 percent of the world's population, the U.S. consumes one-third of the world's processed mineral resources and nonrenewable energy. And as a direct consequence, we also produce approximately one-third of the world's pollution for our own air and water.

Since the beginning of the Industrial Revolution, resource use has followed an exponential growth pattern similar to human growth. Adequate supplies of many important minerals have been exhausted in the United States, and we have turned elsewhere for our sources. Oil is one example. At the time of the 1973 Arab embargo, the United States was importing just over 30 percent of its supplies. By 1990 foreign supplies provided more than 50 percent of domestic American use. Because of U.S. military intervention in the Persian Gulf in 1985 to protect supply, actual cost to American consumers was $495 a barrel after military expenses were included—twenty-eight times the current market price. Similar price escalations followed the Iraqi invasion of Kuwait in 1990, with a predictable American military response.

Although scientists continue to warn that the magnitude of the environmental crisis demands swift and focused attention, the wheels of change grind slowly. Government officials continue to recommend more study and a go-slow policy to avoid unnecessary disruption of the global economy.[10] The year 1994 marked the ninth consecutive year of no significant increase in U.S. fuel economy, but the horsepower and performance (acceleration rate) of American cars has continued to rise. At the same time, national leaders point to the fuel crisis as justification for opening national wildlife refuges to oil exploration and production.

Renewable Resources

If our consumption of nonrenewable resources (our savings inheritance) is excessive, what of our renewable resources? Resources such as timber, fish, wildlife, fresh water, grassland and soil have mechanisms by which they can replenish themselves. But knowledge of their rate of renewal is critical because such rates set the upper limit of our rate of use. If we exploit any resource faster than it can be replenished, we are failing to differentiate between principal and interest, and we will soon have no income left. If our rates are excessive enough, resources which must provide for the needs of our own children can be exhausted before they are old enough to use them.

Soils and forests are a remarkable part of creation. Even small areas of forests or prairies can contain hundreds of species and millions of individual living things, each involved in a dynamic exchange of material and energy with their environment. As surface organisms die, the energy and material stored within their bodies is released by decomposers. Such energy sustains the life of the decomposers themselves, and the materials are returned to the soil as nutrient capital for future use. This decomposition process maintains a proper soil pH and a constant flow of essential minerals required for living members of the system. Earthworms and other invertebrates burrowing through the soil provide passage for air and water movement, both essential for the growth of plants.

Under many natural conditions, the rate of decomposition exceeds or balances the rate of uptake, providing a growing or stable soil system. Thus soils naturally replenish themselves. They are renewable, though their renewal rate is very slow, about one-half inch of topsoil per century under optimal conditions.

Our use of soils does not always consider their self-sustaining properties. A typical American farm provides an excellent example. In order to maximize crop production we increase the natural nutrient supply through fertilization. Farmers used to spread manure on their fields to balance the nutrient drain from the harvest. Manure is organic material, food for the detritus consumers. The chemical fertilizers that have replaced manure, combined with selected biocides to eliminate competition from weeds and insects, damage the soil. The dynamic living system is eliminated and with it the soil's natural ability to sustain itself.

No natural replacement of the soil's nutrient base can occur.

In addition to the loss of living members of the soil system, modern farming practices result in massive amounts of erosion with soil loss often greatly exceeding the annual rate of renewal. The Dust Bowl years should have taught us a powerful lesson. Unfortunately, the erosion rates today often exceed those of the late 1920s and early 1930s. To squeeze out top dollar per acre, farmers often sacrifice both their soils and their future. Today soil is eroded faster than it forms on one-third of the world's cropland. It is estimated that American agricultural land has already lost one-third of its topsoil. This figure often exceeds fifty percent in the corn belt of the American Midwest.

In 1983, farmer Glen Miller was cultivating twenty-one thousand acres west of Colfax, Washington, in the rich Palouse Prairie region of the Pacific Northwest. Regarding conservation practices on his farm, Miller remarked, "If I didn't owe anything, that would be duck soup. I could take those hills and put them all into conservation. . . . But if we use conservation, I can't meet my payments. In the fall they don't ask you what you got in conservation. Creditors don't care where I get the dollars as long as I pay."[11]

Like the patriarch Abraham, Glen Miller does not own any of the land he uses. The only land he owns outright is a pair of cemetery plots. "None of our places is paid for," says Miller. "They're all under mortgage."[12] Abraham was never "under mortgage" because he knew his land was a gift from God. But in modern America, we may be building an unpayable debt to more than the bank. As farmer and author Wendell Berry put it, "By laying up 'much goods' in the present—and in the process using up such goods as topsoil, fossil fuel and fossil water—we incur a debt to the future we cannot repay. That is, we diminish the future by deeds that we call 'use,' but which the future will call 'theft.' "[13]

Only about half of our farms practice soil conservation measures learned during the Dust Bowl era. The loss of topsoil is already being felt in reduced crop yields on many of the most heavily impacted farms. We know how to prevent erosion, but employing contour plowing, terracing, strip cropping and the construction of wind breaks is expensive, and they can reduce production in the short term. Frequently these practices are not employed, especially on large corporate farms where the farm itself can be written off as a tax loss after the soils have been depleted.

But soil loss is not the only tax writeoff. Midwestern farmers pumping water from the Ogallala aquifer (a vast reservoir of groundwater beneath Nebraska, Kansas, Colorado, Oklahoma, Texas and New Mexico) pay nothing extra to deplete this essentially irreplaceable resource. They can, however, claim a depreciation allowance (a tax break) based on the drop in water level beneath their land in that year. The greater the depletion, the greater the allowance.[14]

Like soils, forests are also being consumed more rapidly than they can be replaced. Today we hear much about tropical deforestation. Over half of all known tropical forests have been cleared, and continued cutting removes forests from an area as large as the state of Georgia each year. Studies by researchers David Skole and Compton Tucker, using Landsat satellite imagery, reveal a deforestation rate in Brazilian Amazonia of fifteen thousand square kilometers per year from 1978 to 1988 alone.[15]

Soils and forests are intimately connected. At Manaus, Brazil, one-fourth of all rainfall evaporates directly; half of the rainfall returns to the atmosphere via transpiration from plants; and one-fourth flows into the Atlantic Ocean as runoff. Where land in the same area is deforested, the ratio is reversed. Three-fourths of all water is lost as runoff, and only one-fourth returns to the atmosphere via evaporation and transpiration. Such results initiate a cycle of lower relative humidity, then less rainfall. When the rains do come, there is now no forest to protect the land from erosion, gullying and flash flooding on valuable land which the forest once protected. So the loss of a tropical forest begins to affect both the land and the climate around it.[16]

But deforestation is not limited to tropical countries. Forest loss is occurring in the United States. The U.S. Forest Service, which manages nearly three hundred thousand square miles of forested land, is required by law to harvest on a sustained yield basis. It is mandated to manage the land for five basic priorities. One is timber production, but the others are watershed, minerals, grazing and wildlife/recreation. The Wilderness Society and other conservation organizations in the United States have found evidence that this policy is not being followed. Cutting has often exceeded replacement rate. The recent controversy over old-growth forests and spotted owls in the Pacific Northwest is more than a difference of opinion between lumberjacks and bird lovers. In many ways, the spotted owl controversy has obscured the actual crisis. The real issue of logging in the Pacific Northwest is whether current Forest Service timber management policies are managing old-growth forests on a sustained yield basis. The accumulating evidence is that they are not. Yet the Forest Service has now helped to create a regional economy dependent on cutting the remaining old-growth stands because adequate second-growth stands do not exist.

In September of 1991, John Mumma, then regional forester of the U.S. Forest Service's Northern Region, encompassing fifteen forests and 25 million acres, was forcibly reassigned from his position. Mumma told a packed House subcommittee hearing in Washington, D.C., that he believed his reassignment was a direct result of his failure to meet forest timber harvest targets, targets which Mumma claimed could not be met without breaking federal law.[17]

We must say more of these hearings later (in chapter nine), but we note now that the Mumma hearings depicted the public trusts of our nation's national forests in a state of scandal, of a Forest Service controlled by interests operating outside the boundaries of federal law and of deliberate deception of the public in the enforcement of laws designed to protect the environment.

The Loss of Ecosystems

The demands of an expanding human population for resources and space not only threaten future supplies of needed resources, but also take a heavy toll on ecosystems themselves.

The deserts of North Africa and the Middle East are mute testament to human abuse of the land. Once dominated by forests, they are no longer a land flowing with milk and honey. The cedars of Lebanon are gone. Loss of vegetation and failure to follow the land use laws of Leviticus 25 have modified not only the vegetation but the climate of the entire region.

Tall-grass prairies of North America once supported a rich population of native plants, birds and mammals. Today only about 1 percent of the original prairies remain. Most prairie vegetation that is left is found along rights-of-way of railroad tracks, some freeways and in old rural cemeteries.

The world's wetlands have suffered greatly as human populations have expanded. Important because of their role in wildlife and fish production as well as in flood control and water purification, wetlands are a vital link in the chain of life on earth. Fifty-four percent of original wetlands in the United States have been eliminated, an area four times larger than the state of Ohio. Perhaps 80 percent of this loss has resulted from drainage and subsequent conversion to agriculture. Iowa has lost 95 percent of its marshes, and California 90 percent. Today federal and state laws recognize wetland importance and attempt to preserve important wetland areas, yet estimates indicate that between 300,000 and 450,000 wetland acres continue to be lost each year. Even as this book goes to press, extractive industries and developers renew their efforts to weaken existing laws protecting wetlands at both state and national levels.

The Loss of God's Creatures

What good is a fly or a grasshopper? Why worry if some nasty little bug is eliminated from the face of the earth? Why stop the construction of a multimillion dollar dam for a snail darter? You have got to be kidding! Do these attitudes sound familiar? We've heard them all—in church. It is interesting that people who claim to know God well often have little knowledge or concern for the creatures he made.

Out of sight is not necessarily out of mind. As habitats and ecosystems are destroyed, many kinds of creatures perish with them. The impact may be felt most heavily in tropical countries. Approximately 1.6 million different kinds of animal species have been identified by scientists. Until recently, most authorities assumed that between 4 and 5 million actually existed. The latest studies in the New World tropics have found such enormous species diversity that estimates have had to be revised upward to between 10 and 40 million. Perhaps half of these species might live in the forest canopy. But today it is likely that species which have never been identified or described are being destroyed more rapidly than new ones can be named.

To counter this loss of biodiversity, an effort is currently underway in many countries to establish reserves of various sorts. Approximately

3 percent of U.S. land is managed to protect its natural systems.[18] National wildlife refuges and wilderness areas play primary roles in this effort. Yet more than 230 distinct ecosystems are represented in the United States, each with its own unique assemblage of plants and animals, and only eighty-one are included in the current wilderness preservation system. Without additional efforts aimed at preserving ecosystems currently held in private lands, even a refuge system as extensive as our own will not secure a future heritage for all of God's creatures.

For this effort to be successful, all of the world's major biological communities should be represented by protected areas of sufficient size to maintain their long-term sustainability. On a global scale, the world has been divided into eight biogeographical regions, which in turn have been subdivided into 227 biogeographical provinces. Although all eight regions have some protected areas, fifteen of the provinces have received no protection, and thirty others are inadequately protected (less than one thousand square kilometers).[19]

Today the tiny country of Costa Rica stands out as a world leader in the preservation of resources and biodiversity. With 27 percent of its land designated as parks and reserves, Costa Rica has taken seriously the threat to its national heritage. This single country the size of West Virginia may contain from 5 to 7 percent of all the world's plants and animals.[20] As in most tropical countries, the level of protection varies from one reserve to another. Complete protection is demanded in some areas of extremely high biodiversity.

In other Central and South American countries, another category of rainforest preserves, known as extractive reserves, allows native people to continue to use the forest in nondestructive ways, such as nut gathering, latex harvesting, hunting and limited sustainable logging. In this way productive resources are drawn from the forest, yet most of the species dependent on it remain.

As time passes, those of us living in North America will become acutely aware of the success or failure of tropical efforts to preserve biodiversity. If they do not succeed, our familiar choruses of spring birds will be missing many sections of the choir. Many North American breeding birds depend on tropical forests during winter months. As tropical forests disappear, so will the species that depend on them.

Species we take for granted to reduce crop insect pests and depress biting fly populations may be among the casualties. We can easily calculate the cost of a bottle of insecticide. What is the cost to replace the violet-green swallow or the magnolia warbler?

When the Lord returns and asks us to behold Behemoth, first among the works of God (Job 40:15-24), what if we reply that Behemoth is no more, that he has been destroyed with countless other creatures? To whom much is given, much will be required.

What We Put into God's World

Human impact is not limited to what we take from creation. One of civilization's greatest products, its waste, causes global tears in the fabric of creation. The evening news is a daily reminder of the reality of acid rain, the greenhouse effect, ozone holes, toxic chemicals in air and water, and pollution-related disease.

As we discussed in chapter one, natural ecosystems are largely self-sustaining. The materials they require come from the environment itself. They enter a living system, are used, and eventually released and returned to the system through the action of decomposers. The movement of such material follows predictable pathways, but that does not mean that the specifics are easily understood. That is why the description, measurement and modeling of such cycles remains one of the most active areas of scientific research today. Such research has taken on a new urgency. If in modeling such cycles we can understand their natural path as well as the impacts of superimposed change from human activities, perhaps we can predict the consequences of such changes before it is too late, before the entire pathway of an essential cycle collapses.

Acid Rain

Acid rain is not a local problem, nor is it a new problem. Acid deposition first began to be observed in England in the seventeenth century as the country was deforested, wood became scarce and coal became the primary energy source.[21] The term itself was first used in 1872 by English chemist Robert Angus Smith to describe the rainfall of both England and Germany.[22]

And the problem has grown more international ever since. Acid rain began to be perceived as a problem in Scandinavian countries where, in the late 1950s and early 1960s, scientists noticed increasing acidity levels in lakes and declining fish populations. More rigorous studies in the late sixties and early seventies confirmed conclusively that rain over Scandinavia was becoming more acidic, and that this change was directly related to declining freshwater fish populations.[23]

Pollution produced by one country or state respects no borders. As in Europe, where acid rain falling on Scandinavian soils was actually being generated in England and Germany, much of the acid rain falling on the soils of Canada is generated in the United States. Taller smokestacks were built to reduce the local impact of pollution, but this did not solve the problem. It only succeeded in changing acid rain from a regional issue to one of national and international significance.

The primary source of acid rain is the combustion of fossil fuels. When oil and coal are burned, sulfur is combined with oxygen and released into the air. Burning at high temperatures also causes atmospheric nitrogen to combine with oxygen and results in the release of nitrogen oxides. In the atmosphere, such oxides of sulfur and nitrogen react with water vapor to produce sulfuric and nitric acid. These compounds fall from the sky within rain and snow. Today the average acidity of precipitation falling over the northeastern United States is that of pH 4.5 or below, compared to the 5.6 pH associated with normal rainfall. Rainfall as acidic as pH 2.0 has been recorded at some locations. This means, because the pH scale is logarithmic, that such rainfall is almost ten thousand times more acidic than normal.

This acidification of soil and water is having a major impact. Millions of dollars of damage annually occurs to structures and products of society. Crop damage is becoming evident. The dollar impact on the natural environment, however, is unmeasurable. Thousands of lakes in the United States, Canada and Europe, which a few years ago had thriving fish populations, now have no fish at all. Recent evidence suggests that acid rain may be contributing to the decline of many amphibian species as well.

The impact of acid rain on vegetation is well documented. Several species of trees are suffering severe declines in forests of the northern hemisphere. In 1982, 8 percent of the trees in Germany's Black Forest were dead. A year later the figure was 34 percent. By 1987, 50 percent of the trees were skeletons. Similar problems now appear to be surfacing in forests of the northeastern United States.

Acid rain has become not only an economic issue but also a political one. In 1990 Montana's lieutenant governor and Republican candidate for the United States Senate, Allen Kolstad, told a luncheon of coal company executives that acid rain was "not a problem," that lakes which environmentalists claimed had become fishless through acid rain had never had any fish at all. The media reported Kolstad's statements, and a furor ensued. Kolstad tried to defuse the issue by clarifying his statements and citing his sources, but he refused to change his basic claim that acid rain was not a serious concern. He also refused to provide the media with a written copy of his remarks at the luncheon. When the votes were finally counted, incumbent Democratic senator Max Baucus received 70 percent of the Montana vote, Allen Kolstad 30 percent.

The Greenhouse Effect
"The greenhouse effect" is an expression used today to describe a problem affecting the delicate balance of conditions in the earth's atmosphere which make life possible. Certain gases in the atmosphere act as a kind of gaseous blanket, permitting short-wave radiation from the sun to enter, but intercepting and trapping long-wave heat radiation escaping from the earth. The greater the concentration of these "greenhouse gases," the more heat is retained. Since the beginning of the Industrial Revolution, the concentration of these gases has been increasing. Carbon dioxide is one of the most important gases involved. In any ecosystem, carbon dioxide normally moves from the atmosphere into the plants during the process of photosynthesis. Plants pass the carbon to animals when the plants are eaten, or into the soil when the plant, or parts of the plant, die and decay. From animals and soil, carbon is eventually returned to the atmosphere through respiration and decomposition.

When plant material is placed under sufficient heat and pressure, coal and oil can be formed. When this occurs over a long time period, the result is the accumulation and storage of great reserves of carbon. The burning of coal and oil, along with the destruction of forests, releases this carbon back into the atmosphere in the form of carbon dioxide. Between 1850 and 1960, atmospheric carbon dioxide increased by 25 percent. And in just the last three decades atmospheric carbon dioxide levels have increased approximately 12 to 13 percent.[24] One-fifth of this increase can be reasonably attributed to the destruction of forests, and the other four-fifths to the burning of fossil fuels. In 1987 it was estimated that in Brazil alone some 500 million tons of carbon were released into the atmosphere. Today, carbon dioxide emissions are increasing at the rate of 4 percent per year.

With 57 percent of warming effects attributable to carbon dioxide, it receives most of the attention, but carbon dioxide is only one of several gases contributing to the greenhouse effect. Other contributors include chlorofluorocarbons (CFCs), which are also linked with damage to the ozone layer, and the gases methane and nitrous oxide.

The primary impact of the greenhouse effect is believed to be global warming. If the current levels of carbon dioxide should double (a plausible possibility which could occur between A.D. 2025 and 2100), current state-of-the-art global circulation models (GCMs) all predict an increase of global surface temperatures in the range of 3.5 to 5.2°C.[25] The greatest warming is expected to occur at high latitudes with an accompanying increase in the melting of polar ice.[26] The same GCMs also predict an average surface temperature increase over the central United States in the range of 4 to 6°C (7 to 11°F) during the winter (December-February) and a 3 to 6°C (5 to 11°F) increase during summer (June-August).[27] If average global temperatures increased only 7°F over the next 100 years, sea levels would be expected to increase by 1.6 to 5.0 feet, resulting in large-scale coastal flooding. If this occurred, most low-lying coastal cities, much of southern Florida, the eastern coastal plain of North America and many oceanic islands like the Marshalls and Maldives might be submerged. Today new oil platforms constructed in the North Sea are three feet higher than those built a few years ago in anticipation of rising sea levels.

Increasing global temperatures will also affect global climatic patterns. Impacts on agriculture could be profound. Even average temperature changes as small as 1.8°F could shift agricultural production zones by as much as ninety miles. Prime agricultural land in the American Midwest would become more arid, and grain-producing belts would move northward into Canada.

In Asia, climate change models developed by Australia's national research organization, the CSIRO, predict that eight south Asian countries, which hold one-quarter of the world's population, could face severe economic and environmental disruption as a result of climate change.[28] The Climate Institute, a Washington, D.C.-based think tank, predicts that effects associated with global warming over the next eighty years could produce destruction of fisheries, increased storm damage and the displacement of millions of people. Much of the damage will occur due to weather changes and loss of low-lying land inundated by predicted rises in sea level.[29]

World health officials are concerned that global warming could result in the range expansion of disease-causing parasites. For example, recent computer models indicate the potential for significant spread of *Plasmodium falciparum*, the organism causing the most virulent form of malaria. Other diseases of concern include schistosomiasis, sleeping sickness, and dengue and yellow fevers.

Some recent studies have rightly cautioned against coming to conclusions about global warming that are beyond what present findings can demonstrate. It is understandable that a long-term effect taking place on a worldwide scale can be difficult to document. Because atmospheric temperatures show a normal amount of variation from year to year, it also will take considerable time to show if world temperatures in the present generation are significantly different from those of the past.

These cautions, though they are rightfully expressed, do not minimize the threat to life on earth that can be created when excessive amounts of carbon dioxide are released into the atmosphere. And ominous signals of real climate change are coming in from many fronts. In the Antarctic, two species of flowering plants have dramatically increased in population levels since 1964, the result of an Antarctic growing season that has increased by two weeks over that period.[30] An international group of scientists has detected substantial warming in waters of the subtropical Atlantic.[31] Records of glacier fluctuations compiled by the World Glacier Monitoring Service provide an independent assessment of global warming during the past one hundred years. During that time glaciers have been retreating worldwide.[32] Canadian researchers have found that increased growing season temperatures, combined with the effects of wildfires, are causing deciduous trees to spread north into the Arctic.[33] In addition, there has been a measured and carefully documented rise in sea levels worldwide. The latest studies suggest that this rise is not only an effect of global warming but a result of the draining of aquifers, inland seas and wetlands, and a result of worldwide deforestation.[34]

As ecologist Paul Ehrlich has pointed out, a lack of scientific certainty is not an excuse for inaction. He offers two reasons. First, the kinds of rapid climatic change which some GCMs have predicted under some conditions of global warming would lead to the deaths of millions of people. Even if the chances of this happening were only 10 percent, it warrants action. If you thought there was a 10 percent chance of this book exploding in your hands, you would not be reading it. Second, insuring against the rapid climatic change associated with global warming carries more benefits than costs, including improving energy efficiency, reducing resource consumption and waste, improving air quality and upgrading mass transportation systems.[35]

The Ozone Layer

Depletion of the ozone layer is another area of major concern. Near the earth's surface, ozone is considered a major contributor to air pollution. It can cause eye irritation and respiratory problems, and can harm trees and crops as well as rubber and other materials. But in the stratosphere, ozone is a vital component. It absorbs incoming ultraviolet (UV) radiation and prevents most of it from reaching living things on the surface. It is this UV radiation that is linked to skin cancer and cataracts in humans, as well as significant impacts to nonhuman life which are still poorly understood. It has been estimated that a 10 percent reduction in ozone levels in the earth's upper atmosphere would result in an additional three hundred thousand cases of basal-cell and squamous-cell skin cancers, and an additional fourteen thousand more malignant melanomas.[36]

The harmful concentrations of ozone that can occur near the surface are byproducts of transportation and industry and a component of urban smog. Another product of our industrial society, the previously mentioned CFCs, are now known to destroy stratospheric ozone. The National Aeronautics and Space Administration (NASA) presented evidence in 1988 that a 3 percent reduction in ozone is already evident over North America, Europe and Asia. During winter months there is a 6 percent reduction over Alaska and Scandinavian Europe. By January 1993 the winter decline over northern latitudes had reached 13 to 14 percent.[37] In September 1994 the Ozone Assessment Panel, an international working group of some 226 atmospheric scientists, released a report that confirmed that record ozone depletions have occurred in recent years and were expected to worsen.[38] A NASA press release during the winter of 1994-1995 reported an ozone loss of as much as 40 percent. Efforts to tie the recent rapid decline in ozone levels to the 1991 eruption of Mount Pinatubo in the Philippines have not been successful.

The most notable result of increasing upper-atmosphere CFC concentrations has been the notorious "hole" in the ozone layer that develops over Antarctica during September and October. This reduction in ozone reached record lows in 1991, and again in 1992 and 1993. In a December 19, 1994, press release, NASA stated, "Three years of data from NASA's Upper Atmospheric Research Satellite (UARS) have provided conclusive evidence that human-made chlorine in the stratosphere is the cause of the Antarctic ozone hole."[39]

CFCs constitute a group of chemicals once thought to be entirely safe. They are stable, odorless, colorless, nontoxic, nonflammable and noncorrosive. Their widespread use in industry includes propellant in spray cans, foaming agents in Styrofoam and other plastics used for insulation and packaging, hospital sterilants, and cleaners for electronic parts. They also serve as the coolant in most air conditioners and refrigerators. They are a vital part of a multibillion-dollar industry, and a growing threat to life on earth. Substitutes for CFCs now have been developed by some chemical manufacturing companies and may speed the replacement of CFCs in many applications.

Some have suggested that the ozone problem is no longer cause for concern now that we have banned the use of CFCs as propellants in spray cans and have begun phasing them out of most industrial production. We must remember, however, that nearly all of the existing air conditioners and refrigerators in the world contain CFCs. As these age, leak and are disposed of, what will happen to their CFCs? CFC molecules are lighter than air. Eventually they will enter the stratosphere and reach the ozone layer. There further decomposition of CFC molecules will release chlorine atoms, which will continue to degrade stratospheric ozone. In the stratosphere, chlorine atoms are very stable and will persist for many years.

In short, the CFCs released today will continue to degrade ozone for many years into the future. According to Joe Walters of NASA's Jet Propulsion Laboratory,

> We have basically won a victory for this planet. . . . Sometime after the turn of the century, chlorine is predicted to go down. The question is, Have we done this soon enough? For 100 years, there is going to be as much or more chlorine in the stratosphere as [that which] caused the ozone hole. And it is going to be several centuries before chlorine decays back down to natural levels.[40]

Though the recovery will be slow, the best available current estimates predict that ozone levels will begin making a slow recovery around 1998.[41]

What Creation Demands of Us

Human beings have fulfilled God's command to fill the earth. Perhaps it is full enough. But it is not only, or even primarily, growth that threatens creation. It is consumption. Although more than 90 percent of the world's population growth is occurring in developing nations, it is the industrialized nations that consume a disproportionate share of world resources and strain creation's resources to the breaking point. Current demands on nonrenewable resources threaten to exhaust supplies of many critical materials within present lifetimes. Renewable resources are also threatened as demand exceeds rate of renewal. As we process these materials, the wastes we produce defile air, land and water. Now we must examine more closely the outcomes of these practices.

We must begin to live like stewards. Humans are responsible to God to maintain creation's fruitfulness. It is not primarily for humanity that Adam tends the garden, but for God, the Creator. He is the One who commissioned us as stewards. We have the privilege of using creation's fruitfulness for our own needs, but we dare not forget our responsibility. If our stewardship becomes self-serving, creation's fruitfulness will be diminished and our lives will be impoverished.

Questions for Thought and Discussion

1. How has the physical world around you changed since you were a child? Are there any experiences you had which your children cannot have? Are there any experiences your children have with creation which you did not?

2. How would ecological problems affect missionary efforts and audiences in developing countries? In what ways can missionaries respond to human need created by a deteriorating environment?

3. Of the environmental problems described in this chapter, which one affects you most directly? Is there a way your influence and actions can contribute to a solution to this problem?

8
The Consequences
of Disobedience

*Man has suddenly fallen from God and is still
in flight. The Fall is not enough for him; he
cannot flee fast enough.*
D I E T R I C H   B O N H O E F F E R [1]

E CANNOT CONTINUE TO BASE OUR LIVES ON THE MYTH OF, AS
economist Herman Daly expressed it, "more for all with
sacrifice by none."[2] The present state of God's creation leads
to three inescapable conclusions. First, continued growth of the human population threatens human ability to care for God's creation as
stewards. Second, as a direct result of this growth, nonrenewable
resources are being depleted and renewable resources are being consumed at rates greater than which they can be replaced. Third, the
waste products of human society are overwhelming the earth's ability
to absorb them.

In the midst of its travail, "the creation waits in eager expectation
for the sons of God to be revealed . . . in hope that the creation itself
will be liberated from its bondage to decay and brought into the
glorious freedom of the children of God" (Romans 8:19-21). The
liberation spoken of here is not merely an end to pollution but an
entire renovation and renewal of creation itself. It is an act of God,
and will not be completed until Christ's return. Nevertheless, humans in general, being made in the image of God, and Christians
in particular, being redeemed children of God, bear responsibilities
to begin the redemptive process, caring for and healing creation in

preparation for its final redemption by God.

Before such care can be rightly motivated and carried out, it is important to clearly understand exactly what the consequences are of not carrying it out. Both the past and the present provide abundant examples.

The Biblical Record

We have already examined (in chapter four) some of the impacts of the Fall of humanity upon the physical creation, but we should review them again here. The events of Genesis 3 resulted in a broken relationship between humans and other created things. Human desire to control human destiny shattered the shalom of the created order. No longer was humankind able to lovingly relate to the Creator, nor did the Creator's love and knowledge flow freely to the creature which he had made in his image. And rather than enjoying a creation that produced its crops freely, humankind now found a creation that required painful labor before yielding its fruit.

The evil which humanity released into the world brought God's judgment as a response, and nearly all life was destroyed in the flood. Following this judgment, God established a covenant with the survivors, including the family of Noah. "Never again will all life be cut off by the waters of a flood; never again will there be a flood to destroy the earth" (Genesis 9:11). God provided a rainbow as a sign of the covenant that he made with Noah, his descendants and every living creature. Yet, though the flood was a judgment against evil, it did not purge it from creation. Creation continued to suffer.

Through Moses, God gave the nation of Israel instructions for the care of the land. "When you enter the land I am going to give you, the land itself must observe a sabbath to the LORD. For six years sow your fields, and for six years prune your vineyards and gather their crops. But in the seventh year the land is to have a sabbath of rest, a sabbath to the LORD" (Leviticus 25:2-4). This year of rest allowed soil nutrients to regenerate. Failure to follow the practice would lead to loss of soil fertility. If these instructions were followed, said God, "then the land will yield its fruit, and you will eat your fill and live there in safety" (Leviticus 25:19). Failure to obey these laws was treated as sin, a criminal offense against God. The God-given right to live in the land could be taken away, and the punishment (appropriately) would be exile.

> Then the land will enjoy its sabbath years all the time that it lies desolate and you are in the country of your enemies; then the land will rest and enjoy its sabbaths. All the time that it lies desolate, the land will have the rest it did not have during the sabbaths you lived in it. (Leviticus 26:34-35)

Today many people have the mistaken idea that the Bible is only concerned with "spiritual" things, by which they often mean things that are either sentimental or unreal. This is not true. The Bible is concerned with "spiritual" things in the sense of addressing unseen realities, but it connects them closely to realities which humans can perceive. So it declares that moral offenses against God ("spiritual" sins) have objective consequences in the world around us, not merely in the human mind or in human relationships but also in the nonhuman creation. Isaiah declares:

> The earth dries up and withers,
>> the world languishes and withers,
>> the exalted of the earth languish.
> The earth is defiled by its people;
>> they have disobeyed the laws,
> violated the statutes
>> and broken the everlasting covenant.
> Therefore a curse consumes the earth;
>> its people must bear their guilt.
> Therefore earth's inhabitants are burned up. (24:4-6)

The prophet Hosea is even more explicit: "Because of this [human sin] the land mourns, and all who live in it waste away; the beasts of the field and the birds of the air and the fish of the sea are dying" (4:3).

God's judgments against these actions are not confined to the past. The Bible warns that the final and complete judgment against such activities is reserved for the future. The book of Revelation describes a time "for rewarding your servants the prophets and your saints and those who reverence your name, both small and great—and for destroying those who destroy the earth" (11:18).

The punishment is extreme because God considers such destruction an extreme sin. This is understandable to us when we understand that Christ's death was not merely for humanity, but for creation.

> God was pleased to have all his fullness dwell in him [Christ], and through him to reconcile to himself all things, whether things on earth or things in heaven, by making peace through his blood, shed on the cross. (Colossians 1:19-20)

The Record of History

The Bible's historical record of Israel's land abuse is corroborated by other witness of historical and scientific investigation (as discussed in chapter four). Recent efforts in Israel are aimed at reversing the historical trend of land abuse and making the Judean desert bloom again. The goal of one such effort is to reestablish historical plant communities at a site known as Neot Kedumim, a popular stop on many tours of the Holy Land. Zev Naveh describes it as a "Biblical Nature Reserve in the Judean foothills."[3] The entire area had been severely degraded. There was little left on the surface except bare rock after years of cutting, burning and grazing. However, in the past two decades, major restoration efforts have transformed this wasteland into a vista of landscapes representing those mentioned in biblical and Talmudic literature, the "green heritage" of Jews and Christians alike. Naveh goes on to state that "the restorationists at Neot Kedumim have used the scriptures themselves as a primary source of information in defining their target communities. This is certainly appropriate, especially since the historical accuracy of the Bible is reconfirmed by each new archaeological finding. . . . The reserve serves as a living diorama of the Biblical landscape."[4]

Beyond the Holy Land, recent study of fossil pollen from North African deserts indicates that much of this area was covered by forests only a few thousand years ago. It is believed that humans have played a significant role in the deforestation process.

In the East, China's ecology has undergone profound changes at the hands of humanity. Although ancient written records indicate an awareness of the problems associated with forest loss, most of the former forests are gone. Some were burned according to ancient custom to deprive dangerous animals of needed cover. Others were cleared for agriculture or cut for firewood or charcoal, or for timber consumed in the construction of ancient cities.

The Witness of the Present

Until recently, most actions by humans upon creation were local in their effects. The collapse of the ecological system supporting a city or culture was certainly not insignificant, but creation as a whole felt little impact. In contrast, actions by humans today have global impacts. Resources consumed by industrial societies come from all over the world, and the wastes produced spread over the same environment.

Immense health consequences result. The most personal environment we are called to be stewards of is that of our bodies. Measuring the cost to both personal and corporate health from sexually transmitted diseases, overeating, smoking, alcohol abuse and drug addiction would be beyond calculation. People are literally dying of overindulgence.

Health effects caused by environmental abuse are also mounting. More than four hundred toxic chemicals have now been conclusively linked to human cancer. Studies of disease distribution have shown concentrations of some cancers in areas of industrial and chemical production. Many human birth defects are caused by chemicals known as teratogens. The actual percentage of deformities attributable to teratogens is unknown, but estimates range from 5 to 10 percent. Many chemicals with known teratogenic effects, including polychlorobiphenyls, dioxins, cadmium, mercury and lead, are now present at dangerously high levels in many areas.

A variety of respiratory problems are also known to have environmental origins. The leading cause of lung cancer is air pollution, coming from such specific sources as smoking and inhalation of asbestos fibers. Ozone also damages lung tissue and interferes with the proper functioning of the immune system. Emphysema and bronchitis are also linked with air pollution. Individuals with severe cases are advised to avoid living in cities with bad air quality.

The World Health Organization now estimates that over one billion people are exposed to health hazards from air pollution.[5] In Calcutta, 60 percent of the city's population suffer from respiratory diseases directly related to this problem. Breathing the air in Bombay, on the other side of the Indian subcontinent, is equivalent to smoking ten cigarettes per day.[6] Even in the United States, the American Lung Association estimates that up to 120,000 Americans die from air pollution each year.[7]

The Economic Consequence

Jesus told a story of a certain rich man who laid up an abundance of goods for many years and then believed that he could eat, drink and be merry. But that very night brought the event of his death, and God said to him, "You fool! This very night your life will be demanded from you. Then who will get what you have prepared for yourself?" (Luke 12:20). Jesus concluded, "This is how it will be with anyone who stores up things for himself but is not rich toward God" (v. 21).

In commenting on this parable, author Wendell Berry notes that the rich man's crime seems to be that he has belittled the future, reducing it to the size of his own hopes and aspirations, rather than God's. He is prepared for a future in which he will be prosperous, not for one in which he will be dead. Berry concludes, "We may say, then, that we seek the kingdom of God, in part, by our economic behavior, and we fail to find it if that behavior is wrong."[8]

When any group of individuals fails to properly care for creation, the cost is passed to the public and to the generations of the future. The cost is felt in greater health care expenses, higher taxes and falling property values when the environment around us is filled with dirty air and water. Physical impacts take the form of damage to structures and materials, reduction in commercial fishery catches (with resulting layoffs and unemployment), reduced growth rates in forests, lower crop production and declining recreational tourism in impacted areas. Estimating exact costs is difficult. Our economic system does not track such costs well, and they are easily passed on to the consumer. But intelligent estimates of specific damage are possible. Damage in the United States from acid rain and snow is now estimated at between six and ten billion dollars annually and is expected to rise sharply in the future.[9] Legislation to reduce acid deposition is now in place, but cleaning up will not be cheap. The Environmental Protection Agency (EPA) estimates that it will cost four billion dollars per year to implement the acidic deposition component of the Clean Air Act of 1990.[10]

The production of hazardous and toxic chemicals is considered a normal part of chemical production in the manufacture of many modern products. The final product itself is often environmentally harmless, like computers, solar cells or prescription medicine. Yet some of the chemicals used in their production can have disastrous environmental impact if not properly stored and handled. The results of past mismanagement still haunt us today.

The EPA estimates that the cost to clean up current hazardous waste sites identified under the now infamous Superfund program will be about $77 billion.[11] Yet even that is not the whole cost. The Office of Technology Assessment estimated in 1985 that the final list of toxic waste sites may include at least ten thousand separate locations and cost up to $500 billion over the next fifty years.[12]

The wreck of the *Valdez* in Alaskan coastal waters not only created an environmental disaster of massive proportions, but has cost Exxon and the federal government over three billion dollars in cleanup costs to date, and the effort is far from over. In light of consequences like these we can understand the words of German chancellor Helmut Kohl, who said to William K. Reilly, then head of the U.S. Environmental Protection Agency, "The economy must adapt to environmental priorities, not just as political necessity, but as a matter of morality."[13]

The Aesthetic Impact

It is difficult to place a dollar value on a thousand miles of unspoiled shoreline. Perhaps it is not even proper. But along such shorelines in Alaska which suffered the brunt of the *Valdez* catastrophe it is a real question, made poignant in a surf that casts the carcasses of dead eagles, sea otters and starfish onto oil-covered sands. The year following the spill the whales did not return. Fishermen wonder if the salmon catch will be reduced in the long run. Native Americans ask if the harvests they collect from these waters and these shores will still sustain them. In many sections of the coastline Exxon has claimed that the job is done, but oil has seeped four feet beneath the sand and gravel of the shore in many of these same places, and a sterile waste is the result.

Sometimes I ask my students where they go to find peace of mind and heart when the pressures of life seem to have reached the breaking point. Answers vary, but they have common themes: a peaceful valley, a quiet beach, a forest glen. No one has ever mentioned a factory, an industrial park or an urban street corner.

American essayist H. L. Mencken, commenting on the environment within the city of Pittsburgh at the turn of the century, wrote, "Here was the very heart of industrial America, the center of its most lucrative and characteristic activity, the boast and pride of the richest and grandest nation on earth—and here was a scene so dreadfully hideous, so intolerably bleak and forlorn that it reduced the whole aspiration of man to a macabre and depressing joke."[14]

Is it right that we must run away from human society to find the peace we seek? Would it not be better to transform the human condition into something better? Christ's commission to us is to "Go into all the world and preach the good news to all creation" (Mark 16:15), or as Matthew records it, "Go and make disciples of all nations" (Matthew 28:19). If we would teach the mandates of Scripture, we would not ignore the practice and instruction of the care of God's creation, because we would not fail to point out that the first task of humanity was to till and keep a garden.

In this area of obedience to God, our task is to restore this garden to the splendor God desired for it. Gardening has many tasks and takes many forms. But unless you participate in its care, you do not share in the harvest (1 Corinthians 9:7). What have you done to help tend the Lord's garden today?

The Cost to Culture

Chico Mendez is a national hero in Brazil. He was also a martyr. A native rubber tapper whose livelihood and culture were threatened by the conversion of forest to grazing land by powerful cattle barons, Chico became a national symbol of the resistance movement. Through the efforts of Chico and others, the Brazilian government began to reexamine its land use policy. After a trip to North America and meetings at the United Nations and the World Bank, Chico Mendez returned to Brazil, a hero to his people. A few months later he was murdered.

Such politically motivated murders are not uncommon in South America, where issues of land reform are at stake. Not only individuals are at risk, but whole tribes and nations of native people. Each of these has a unique knowledge of its surroundings which has permitted its members to live in harmony with their environment for hundreds or thousands of years.

I met Otto on a trip to South America a few years ago during a course I was teaching on tropical ecology. He lives with his family along a river called the Río Napo and was our host for a week. As he guided us along the hidden paths of a rainforest he knew so well, he spoke of the medicinal value of one kind of plant after another. White latex sap from a vine he showed me rids the body of intestinal parasites. Leaves from a small tree reduce high blood pressure. Some in our group were suffering from severe intestinal distress. Otto had them eat the crushed leaves from another plant. The symptoms rapidly disappeared.

Perhaps no one knows the full extent of the knowledge these native peoples have about their environment. A cure for Hodgkin's disease comes from a rare plant in Madagascar. The sap of a tree in Brazil can be burned as diesel fuel. The list is long, but the knowledge could be easily lost. A culture so closely connected to its environment will be destroyed if that environment is destroyed. Already many such cultures, and their knowledge, have passed away in the wake of tropical rainforest destruction. And their like will not be seen again in this creation.

A very real example of the impact of Western society on an isolated Amazon tribe was provided one day in January 1995. On that day I sat on the floor of Victoriano's home on the bank of the Río Cuyabano in Ecuador. Victoriano is the seventy-eight-year-old chief of the Siona Indians. I was again in South America with a group of American students from my college. We were five hours upriver from the nearest road. That morning we had seen an odd sheen on the waters of Laguna Grande near our camp. Victoriano was clearly troubled when he told us that another group of Siona Indians recently had asked if they could move their village into his territory. They said their land and river had become so polluted by the oil from Texaco's exploitation of nearby oil reserves that no food remained, and survival was impossible. United States laws regulating oil extraction in our own country do not cross our borders, and international laws do not exist. Ecuador is a developing country with few environmental laws and even less ability to enforce them. The Ecuadorian subsidiary of Texaco was asked to leave the country, and Ecuador filed suit to collect for environmental damage. The company countered by filing bankruptcy.

The Disobedience of the Church
The results of a significant research study were published in 1980 by Stephen Kellert and Joyce Berry of Yale University. Their work was part

of a study funded by the U.S. Fish and Wildlife Service to determine knowledge and attitudes of Americans toward their environment. Data were collected from carefully prepared surveys returned by thousands of Americans from across the country. One of Kellert and Berry's questions dealt with the frequency of attendance at religious services. The results indicated that those with the highest attendance at such services had the lowest knowledge of environmental concerns. Using responses from a number of different questions to assess the general attitude of the respondent to the environment, Kellert and Berry also found that those who attended church services most regularly had the most dominionistic and utilitarian attitudes toward the creation around them.[15]

In chapter three we discussed the traditionally popular view of blaming the present environmental crisis on a Judeo-Christian view of the world, articulated by Berkeley historian Lynn White Jr.[16] That argument is seriously flawed in both its exegesis of Scripture and its interpretation of historical data. Yet the findings of Kellert and Berry support White's contention that at least among present churchgoers, the church has imparted an attitude that God's creation exists for them to dominate and use for their own purposes.

This book, among others, documents the extensive biblical witness to the importance of human care of creation. But Western theology has not brought this message to ordinary Christians. For hundreds of years the church has been largely silent on issues relating to creation. Today both the church and the Christian must face difficult questions. Do they have a different attitude toward the care of creation from that of non-Christian institutions and individuals? Are Christians and their churches more knowledgeable or more involved in environmental issues? Do either participate more actively in environmental organizations and decisions?

Lynn White Jr. correctly pointed out decades ago that the problems of our ecologic crisis are problems of worldview, not merely of science or technology. He was correct in stating that the problem is a religious one. To most people living in Western society, nature and God are historically related. They believe that God created nature. They believe that God exists and is primarily concerned with his relationship to humanity, and that nature exists to provide for human need. This is sometimes identified as a religious view. It is not a biblical one.

While some segments of Western Christianity have recently begun to include creation as a significant part of their theology,[17] religions like the New Age movement and Creation Spirituality have made it a major focus. Some popular Christian writers who continue to deny any meaningful theology of creation have gone so far as to label Christians working to preserve creation as proponents of New Age heresies.[18] In reality, the vacuum left by the church's failure to address the creation has provided an issue which helped give birth to the New Age movement. Biologist Richard Wright calls this the "Cyrus Principle." Wright contends, persuasively, that as the Persian (and pagan) king Cyrus was used by God to accomplish his work, so the disobedience of Christians in the care of creation has led to God's use of unbelievers to carry out these commands.[19]

The Difference in Us and the Difference It Makes

Amidst the growth of a Christian environmental ethic and of Christian environmentalists, reflective believers are sometimes troubled by a disturbing question: What is the difference between the Christian environmentalist and the secular environmentalist? What is the difference between Christian environmental ethics and secular environmental ethics? The question reminds me of the title page of a book on "Christ-centered dieting" that my wife was using to lose weight. When I asked what Christ-centered dieting was, she replied, "Oh, it's basically like Weight Watchers, just add prayer and fellowship." But if Christian environmentalism is nothing but the Sierra Club with prayer and fellowship, does the world really need it?

This troubling question, and the doubts that go with it, must be faced. There is, if nothing else, a difference in motivation and belief between Christians and non-Christians. But if that is the only difference, then where is the reality of faith in action? If the Christian ecologist *acts* exactly like the non-Christian ecologist, in word and deed, then what has the knowledge of God added to saving our planet? This question both deserves and demands an answer. And the answer comes as a shock to believers and unbelievers alike. To reach it, we must work backward, following the path and the impacts of secularism through the history of the modern environmental movement.

A Secular Land Ethic

Theologian Alexander Schmemann has defined secularism as, ultimately, the negation of worship.[20] And so it is. It is not that secularism
denies the existence of God. It may be perfectly ready to accept the
premise of his existence. But what secularism can never acknowledge
is the *relation* between humans and God, nor can it ever acknowledge
humans or the world as a *creation* of God. Therefore the world and its
events may inform and direct right action, but religion never can. Since
the beginning of the twentieth century this is the only mode in which
scholars of the state universities have been allowed to think. The only
accepted form for expressing ideas has been the negation of God and,
with that, the "expansion" of ethical boundaries by building a scientifically informed worldview.

Aldo Leopold, living and writing during the desert of intellectual
despair which marked the 1930s and 1940s, understood well how to
survive in this wasteland. He attempted to redefine an ethic for the
land, first by showing what he believed to be the ethical deficiencies of
the Judeo-Christian tradition, and then by remedying those deficiencies from an ecological vantage point. "The land ethic," wrote Leopold,
"simply enlarges the boundaries of the community to include . . .
collectively, the land."[21]

Leopold's magnum opus, *A Sand County Almanac,* is an achievement
of consummate literary skill. Its beauty of expression has made it a
classic of the environmental movement. Yet from an analytical standpoint Leopold never succeeded in delivering a defined ethic within the
pages of its text. It was not his skills at definition and debunking that
were at fault. In definition, Leopold rightly states that an ethic is a
differentiation between social and antisocial behavior; in the ecological
sphere, this is a limitation on the freedom of action in the struggle for
existence.[22] As for debunking, Leopold subscribed to the then-popular
view that ethics had "evolved" from simpler to more advanced forms.
He considered the "Mosaic Decalogue" (Leopold never referred to
them by their more popular appellation, the Ten Commandments) as
an early example of a "simple" ethic for relations between individuals,
and the golden rule an advancement that attempted to integrate the
individual to society. Democracy, to Leopold, represented a still more
advanced ethic in which social organization was integrated to the needs

of the individual. In such an ethical evolution, the final step would be the "land ethic." Leopold believed that such an ethic would change "the role of *Homo sapiens* from conqueror of the land community to plain member and citizen of it. It implies respect for his fellow members, and also respect for the community as such."[23]

These are beautiful words and noble goals, but on what basis is this respect to be afforded? What gives the land a value great enough to preserve it, even against short-term selfishness? People are not going to save the world for the sake of ecological courtesy. So what makes nature worth saving?

This question did not escape Leopold. He recognized intuitively that ethics based on traditional economic conservation, an ethic based on monetary value, would not do. "One basic weakness in a conservation system based wholly on economic motives," he wrote, "is that most members of the land community have no economic value. Of the 22,000 plants and animals native to Wisconsin [Leopold's home state], it is doubtful whether more than five percent can be sold, fed, eaten, or otherwise put to economic use."[24]

Leopold attempted to move beyond economics by introducing the concept of ecological rights. "These [nonhuman] creatures are members of the biotic community," he wrote, "and if (as I believe) its stability depends on its integrity, they are entitled to its continuance."[25] But who has entitled them?

Leopold's logic can be understood thus:

Premise 1: Living things are a part of the biotic community.

Premise 2: Community (ecological) stability depends on its integrity (the persistence of the community's component parts).

Conclusion: All species that are members of any biotic community must be preserved.

But Leopold's conclusion is not logically valid. We can't draw an imperative conclusion from a subjunctive premise. Nor would any competent philosopher contend that mere existence provides sufficient moral obligation to preserve what does exist. But Leopold is not at this point being analytical. He is simply disguising (knowingly or unknowingly) a form of anthropocentrism that is at the heart of all secular ethics. In such ethics, the real measure of all things is humankind, so human beings may impart value to whatever they will. It is really humankind's survival, not the ecosystem's, that Leopold is ultimately concerned with. And the anthropocentric rat insistently keeps poking its head out of the hole despite Leopold's best attempts to disguise the rat as something else. For example, in defending wilderness preservation, Leopold claims that wilderness is "the raw material out of which man has hammered the artifact of civilization." Wilderness should be preserved "for the edification of those who may one day wish to see, feel, or study the origins of cultural inheritance."[26]

This is where the best of secular ethics must inevitably end, eloquent but unconvincing, inflated with the pride of building its own world but utterly unable to place that world in meaningful relation to anything else.

The conclusion that the Leopoldian land ethic has failed to achieve its professed goals is not merely a personal opinion. James Shaw, a professor in the Department of Zoology at Oklahoma State University, assessed the impact of the Leopoldian land ethic in a 1987 article entitled "Assessing the Progress Toward Leopold's Land Ethic." His article was published in a special volume of *The Wildlife Society Bulletin* in a year commemorating the fiftieth anniversary of the Wildlife Society (an organization founded by Leopold). Shaw writes: "If the land ethic has taken root in the way envisioned by Leopold, its effects are far from evident. . . . Land use practices are still dictated largely, and in many cases solely, on the expectation of short-term economic returns."[27] Shaw goes on to note that the wildlife profession does not "seem to discuss the land ethic very much or seem motivated to analyze progress toward its attainment."[28] He writes that a 1982 symposium on wildlife and land use did not even mention the land ethic and that three recent wildlife-management textbooks also failed to allude to it.

Ultimately Shaw concludes that Leopold's land ethic fails because it relies too much on social pressure rather than on economic and government coercion.[29] But Shaw fails to note that this problem in turn stems from a secularized government, a government that has deemed it inappropriate even to discuss questions of values and ethics because such values and ethics are deeply rooted in religious tradition. When such a tradition—the only genuine basis for personal ethics—fails, coercion is the only option left.

The Search for a Spiritual Land Ethic

So secularism marches, or perhaps stumbles, on—able to perceive the problem, unable to conceive the solution. Yet in the last few decades chinks have appeared in its armor. Its weaknesses began to be revealed with the publication of Lynn White Jr.'s essay "The Historical Roots of Our Ecologic Crisis."

We have said much of this essay elsewhere, and not all of it favorable. Like Leopold, White followed the professionally acceptable path of demonstrating the inadequacies of the Judeo-Christian tradition, and he concluded that such a tradition was the ultimate ground of the ecologic crisis. Unlike Leopold, White did not fall into the trap of trying to construct an alternative from strictly "scientific" sources. Rather, he concluded, "More science and more technology are not going to get us out of the present crisis."[30] Specifically, in his essay White did three things which undermined the secular grip on environmental thinking: (1) he repudiated merely technological solutions to the environmental crisis; (2) he demonstrated that human actions were ultimately grounded in religious conviction, not merely scientific, political or social thinking; and (3) he raised issues about the treatment of the environment which could only be addressed from religious sources. White did great harm to the credibility of Judeo-Christian thinking, but in so doing he had linked religious issues to environmental issues. The battle was joined.

The growing disenchantment with secularism was swelling before "Historical Roots" had gone to press, and it continued to swell thereafter. The inadequacies of purely technical thinking about the environment surfaced more visibly with every passing year.

In a recent interview Cal DeWitt, director of the Au Sable Institute of Environmental Studies and one of the authors of the book *Earthkeeping: Christian Stewardship of Natural Resources,* was asked if he thought an emphasis on nonhuman creation might cause people to lose sight of humanity's unique standing. DeWitt replied,

> That's like putting up a bird feeder and thinking we'll wind up worshiping robins. As people continue to harmonize with nature without professing God, we'll see an increase in Satanic approaches to revering the earth. The solution to the problem is not further isolation from God's creation, but a powerful witness to the one true

God. If we stand back and no longer profess God as Creator, we will see a resurgence of paganism from those in the environmental movement we've abandoned.[31]

Indeed, that is already happening. The environmental movement has ceased to be merely a scientific and technical debate and has become a spiritual journey. Such developments are well described by Alston Chase in his book *Playing God in Yellowstone*. In a chapter entitled "The California Cosmologists," Chase vividly depicts the modern environmental movement's desperate search for transcendent meaning and values beyond mere science and management:

> Like a swarm of bees turned loose in a greenhouse they buzzed around a flowerbed of exotic religions and an eclectic cornucopia of offbeat ideas—Tao, Hinduism, Zen Buddhism, . . . Gnosticism, Manicheanism, Vedanta, Sufism, Cabalism, Spinozistic Pantheism, . . . Yoga, biofeedback, transcendental meditation, Gandhian pacifism, animism, panpsychism, alchemy, ritual magic, . . . Buddhist economics, fossil love, planetary zoning, . . . deep ecology, shallow ecology, reinhabitation, . . . ecosophy, ecological primitivism, feminist physics, chicken liberation, Earth National Park, stone-age economics, . . . Yin Yang and the androgenous universe, Gaia, global futures, Spaceship Earth, . . . the rights of rocks, ecological resistance . . .[32]

And the list goes on.

This desperate search for transcendent meaning and value in the wasteland of secularism has led to the development of the so-called Deep Ecology[33] movement. The advocates of Deep Ecology espouse not a scientific but a religious position, a position characterized not by its ecologic integrity but by its rejection of all things modern and material.[34] But this only serves to highlight the present crisis of secular environmental ethics.[35] The question "What is humanity's place in nature?" cannot be satisfactorily answered by Deep Ecology or New Age spirituality. The failure of the church to address this question has created a vacuum which such movements exploit, but it remains a question that only the church can answer.

The dissatisfaction, and in some cases disgust, with secularism has come to its present head in the Gaia hypothesis, a theory that the earth's lower atmosphere functions, through a series of feedback systems, as a self-regulating, self-sustaining organism. In more scientific language, scientists Stephen Schneider and Penelope Boston state that

> the *Gaia hypothesis* . . . [is that] life has a greater influence on the evolution of the Earth than is typically assumed across most earth science disciplines, but also that life serves as an active control system. . . . [These ideas] suggest that life on Earth provides a cybernetic, homeostatic feedback system, leading to the stabilization of global temperature, chemical composition, and so forth.[36]

Though the hypothesis itself can be considered reasonably scientific, it has spawned a host of ideas and philosophies which reach out to deify the earth. The church must reject idolatry in all its forms, but it must not fail to see, and to see with compassion, what such yearnings represent. As Paul told the people at Corinth, "You were led astray by dumb idols. However, you were led."

The hunger for the divine is a yearning in the human spirit that simply refuses to be argued, analyzed, intimidated or even beaten into submission. And the shallowness of secularism will not pass as a substitute for ethics which must address both the human condition and the moral nature of the ecologic problem. As the character Ellen Linsgaard asks a secularist in George MacDonald's novel *Thomas Wingfold, Curate*, "If there is no God, how is it that I have come to need one?" And as Aldo Leopold noted, the logic of history, as well as the present crisis, demands real bread. It will not accept any more secular stones.

A Christian Ethic: Stewardship of Creation

So we return to our earlier question, "What is the difference between the secular and Christian versions of being an environmentalist?" The answer, surprisingly, is worship. In worship we do not escape the world but rather stand in it, in its very center, at once thanking God for it and offering it back to God as his own creation and possession, and ourselves as creatures in it.

The secular world around us, for all its busyness and noble purpose, is starved for contemplation. It is desperately seeking transcendence, a meaning and purpose for its ceaseless activity beyond itself and its own survival. The secular world starves because it cannot worship. Christians live because we can worship. And the work of restoring a blighted earth has meaning when it can be offered as witness, service, vocation and sacrament to God.

It is the ethical and moral starvation force-fed to modern culture by secularism that is the ultimate blight on the human spirit and the most serious of all the consequences of human disobedience to God. Lynn White Jr. concluded his essay with a call to treat Francis of Assisi as "the patron saint of ecologists" because of his unique "pan-psychism" (White's phrase) in viewing creatures other than humans as having souls.[37] Even if this is what Francis really believed, and that is doubtful, a better model for us would be Jesus himself.

Imagine yourself and some of your friends sitting in the back yard, engaged in casual conversation. Suddenly Christ walks through the gate. He drops to one knee and scoops up a handful of earth. He moistens the soil in his hand and forms it into the shape of a creature, one that has never been before. He draws it close to his face and breathes upon it, and a miracle takes place before your eyes. The lump of soil springs up a living creature; a new creation is added to the living. Then Christ turns to you and places it in your hand, and suggests that you give it a name and provide it with care and love. As quickly as he came, his shadow has passed through the gate, and he is gone.

Today the church must decide whether it will be, to use Wendell Berry's terms, an *exploiter* of creation or a *nurturer* of it. Exploiters are specialists whose concern is efficiency and whose goal is profit. Nurturers are generalists whose concern is care and whose goal is health— their own, their community's and their land's. Exploiters ask of creation, "How much and how quickly?" Nurturers ask, "How well and how long?" In other words, what can creation produce *dependably?* The exploiter wants to earn as much as possible with as little work as possible. The nurturer wishes to earn what is needful and to work as well as possible.[38] Only in nurturing is there stewardship. Only in stewardship is there witness. Only in the rejection of secularism and the embrace of genuine worship can real witness grow.

Human beings do have a special dominance. Failure to affirm this is not only a denial of Scripture but a denial of the world around us. But all created things remain good, and not just good for us. As ethicist James Gustafson has noted, "Special dominance implies special accountability as much as special value."[39] Human dignity arises within creation, not against it.

The charges of Adam now number perhaps thirty million species strong. The tasks of Adam for their care have not changed but have been made more urgent and more difficult because we must now carry out this task within a fallen nature in a sinful world, instead of a sinless nature in a perfect garden. The reports on our evening news of acid rain, ozone depletion and species extinction do not merit either apathy or despair, but response—a response driven by the question "What would Jesus do?"—and the will to carry out the answer.

Questions for Thought and Discussion

1. In what ways do you see spiritual realities manifested or foreshadowed in creation? In what ways is human disobedience to God seen or expressed in creation?

2. What factors have led Christians in America to have dominionistic and utilitarian attitudes toward creation? Is this a biblically informed view? Why or why not?

3. In what ways could you address, from a Christian perspective, human desires to have a better relationship with the creation? In what ways could you demonstrate greater nurturing of creation and less exploitation of it?

9

A Christian Response
Restoration & Redemption

Since the church, at its base, stands or falls on God's willingness to justify the ungodly, it is mistaken to demand that impeccability be a requirement for ethical witness.
R O Y J . E N Q U I S T[1]

BOTH INDIVIDUAL AND CORPORATE RESPONSES ARE NEEDED TO bring about the restoration and redemption of our created world. By now you have probably developed a persistent question: "What should I do about this?"

In everything, the Christian must grow to be a person guided by a personal ethic driven by obedience to God. Choices may differ among individuals. The goal must be the same. What we say in this chapter is not meant to cover every environmental choice one can make. The spectrum of practical choices has been well documented by others. But we do wish to give some examples of how serious consideration of God as Creator and the world as his creation might find expression in the Christian life.

The Individual Response
As we gain more knowledge on any particular topic it usually leads to better understanding and appreciation of the broader context of the subject. Often it alters our way of thinking and creates in us the potential for change in both thought and life. Yet, as we have noted earlier, the Christian will not be marked on this issue primarily by differences in activity. The *activity* of many in the world who make no

claim to be Christians is characteristically intelligent, perseverant, constructive and, we could even dare to say, *redemptive* toward the environment. Yet for all this activity, the world desperately seeks something beyond itself. It is starved for contemplation, meaning and purpose.

For this reason a constructive Christian response begins with something that many people do not consider activity at all. It begins with worship. This worship is the worship of our Creator, but it is not an escape from the world. Worship is that point at which we stand in the world, right in the center of it, receive it thankfully from God and offer it back with gratitude to God. In worship we recognize that the world is God's and that the death and resurrection of Jesus Christ will change not only our own lives but the very cosmos and creation in which we will live them, making not only a new heaven but a new earth. In worship we recognize that salvation is not simply about taking us to God's world (heaven) but a preparation for God's coming to our world (earth) and claiming it for himself, by right of creation.

Thus the first Christian response is worship. Some have expressed the fear that concern for God's creation could lead to a worship of creation, but God's guidance through his Word and his Spirit directs us instead to worship the Creator (Romans 1:25).

Out of worship comes the Christian response to rule creation rightly—humbly but enthusiastically. The authority of ruling is made effective by informed study, deliberate contact and sacrificial concern.

Informed study means that we respond by a determined effort to know more of creation and its needs. It is reflected in money spent to join responsible scientific and conservation organizations and the time it takes to read their publications. We cannot give more than we get. Each household should subscribe to at least one magazine that focuses on and illuminates problems of the environment with well-written articles.

Informed study is manifested in the effort of attending public meetings in which information about creation, specifically the neighborhood creation, is presented and discussed. It is made evident in searching out sources of information—television programs, newspapers, books and magazines—that reveal the conditions and needs of the environment to us.

Deliberate contact means taking ourselves out of our homes, automobiles, shopping malls, sports coliseums and theme parks and into the living world. It is the cultivation of activities like hiking, walking, running, biking, boating, camping, gardening, canoeing, kayaking, photography, hunting, fishing, mountain climbing, botanizing, birdwatching and hundreds more that show us what creation is like, enriching our experiences and revealing the lives of creatures to us in personal ways.

Sacrificial concern is the Christian's directed release of informed study and deliberate contact into action that matters. It means acts of service and support to secure the needs of nonhuman life. It is expressed by tax check-offs for wildlife; buying an acre of marsh; restoring parks, wetlands and woods; planting trees; building brush piles for rabbits. Many organizations seek funds to investigate and prosecute violation of environmental law, to purchase land for preservation and wise management, and to support lobbying activities for environmental legislation. It is not possible to invest in all these things, but it must be a priority to contribute some portion of the family budget to this kind of work. Where your treasure is, there will your heart be also.

Finally, we cannot rule out the possibility that sacrificial concern might mean becoming a steward yourself, as a biologist, botanist, politician, teacher, forester, wildlife manager, hydrologist or environmental engineer. Or it might mean giving your blessing, encouragement and support to a daughter or son who says, "This is what God wants me to do." Sacrificial concern is shown by every act of service to those we rule. For some, the appropriate act of service will be their life and career. For those who give these things gratefully to God, their sacrifice will not seem burdensome.

The Social Contract
We feel safe in assuming that no one reading this book is a hermit. We live among others, and our words and deeds are observed. And those who speak and act with integrity always persuade those who want to live with integrity. How does a Christian response to God's creation extend beyond ourselves?

It might begin with sharing these insights with a friend, neighbor or business acquaintance. It might continue by writing letters to newspapers that everyone sees and reads. It is lobbying legislators to provide protection for wild things and wild places. In local newspapers, letters to the editor are widely read, and elected representatives need to receive personal letters about your interest in the control of pollution, protection of clean water supplies and preservation of natural areas.

We extend a Christian response to God's creation when we begin to use less and save more. Those who recycle their own bottles and cans live with integrity. Those who persuade the city council to make recycling part of the normal garbage-collection procedure have changed their world. The reason to recycle materials or to compost leaves goes beyond compliance with local ordinances. It is within compliance of greater ordinances, cycles that God created for the world in which we live. The relational knowledge that humans and other creatures share a common Creator leads to a deeper understanding of the value of creation.

In making such a response we recognize the need to consider changing long-standing habits and practices. For many years the church has advocated personal piety and purity, often through a list of prohibitions of worldly activities. To this can be added a list of positive actions that are environmentally sensitive and sensible. A lavish, profligate life not only is sinful in the traditional sense, it also uses an unjust portion of resources, a robbery of both the present and future generations. A moderate lifestyle, sensitive to resource use, conserves both time and money for service to others.

Family Involvement

Most people live in families, and most families in neighborhoods. What one individual thinks or does is often noted and talked about by others. Particularly visible in this regard is the way in which energy is used for transportation and for heating. Bicycle use is growing in many areas. In many places, traffic lanes exclusively for bicycles have been added and developed on miles of roads and trails. As commuting by car continues to try the patience of drivers with traffic jams and gridlock, the bicycle may well come into more frequent use for getting to and from work. Family outings on bicycles redeem more time for interaction and waste less time in stalled traffic lanes.

The family vacation itself can become an activity more sensitive to

God's creation. Vacations from the routine of daily life are a needed change for rest and relaxation. But perhaps a jet flight overseas is not the best alternative. A driving vacation within reasonable distances from home can accomplish the same objective at less cost to the creation and the pocketbook. The selection of the automobile itself is a powerful choice among your environmental options. More miles per gallon means less harmful emissions as well as less gas cost to you. And vehicles designed for higher alcohol-gasoline ratios have less emissions still. The alcohol itself can be produced from the byproducts of agriculture, and its substitution for gasoline may someday reduce the cost of the constant search for oil. Electric cars are another option that consumers must begin to demand, along with the continued development and improvement of mass-transit systems.

The wise use of energy in heating water and homes is another area where family commitments make a world of difference in both the short and the long term. Insulating water jackets can be added to existing water heaters in the "do it now" category, and solar water heating can be incorporated in new homes. Visitors to Israel and Cyprus often comment on the many rooftop solar water heaters in use there. In the United States, some urban areas, like San Diego, have enacted ordinances requiring solar water heaters in all new housing construction. Planning for energy conservation in the design and construction of homes has improved considerably in the last two decades, but much more could be done with federal incentives and subsidies.

Even the retrofitting of older homes can lead to energy savings. One of us has installed an eleven-hundred-gallon water tank in the basement of his home. It functions as an integral part of supplementary home heating as well as a component of the central air conditioning system in summer. In winter, not only does the fire in the fireplace add to the pleasure of a good book, but water flowing through the pipes in the grating absorbs heat from the fire, which is then stored in the basement tank. A water-to-air heat pump then extracts the heat and channels hot air to the regular furnace fans. In the summer the heat pump is switched to take cold air from the tank of cool water and circulate it through the home. The tank heats up during the day, so at night water is pumped outside to an evaporator near the ground. In this way the water tank begins the next day with cool water. This system was installed during the late 1970s, and it has provided savings of money and energy to the present time with very little maintenance.

It is at the family level that values, including attitudes and practices toward the environment, are best taught by actions that illustrate the truth of our words. Children raised in a home where recycling, energy conservation and respect for God's creation are practiced will find these ways of life easier to adopt themselves as they grow to adulthood. Not all will choose this path, but the correct choices are easier to see if they are instructed by parents seeking "to do justice, to love kindness, and to walk humbly with [their] God" (Micah 6:8 NASB).

At both individual and family levels, participation in community activities is a natural outlet for communicating values and interests related to environmental themes. Volunteers are often needed at the local recycling center. Summer day camps include units on nature study. County fairs and annual parades seek participation by individuals and families representing church and civic organizations. Concern and care for the earth are visible themes that can be publicly portrayed and proclaimed in all these settings. A local case in point was the recent formation of the organization "Partners for Lincoln Marsh" in Wheaton, Illinois. The group's volunteers work under the direction of the city park district to preserve and develop a wetland for conservation and education even in the midst of suburban Chicago. Trails have been established, boardwalks installed and a water clarification project initiated. The blueprints for a new environmental learning center have been drawn up, to be built at the edge of the marsh along the historic Illinois Prairie Path.

Grassroots projects like this abound throughout the country, and their numbers are increasing. Perhaps most significant is the formation of the Society of the Green Cross, an organization of evangelical Christians dedicated to proclaiming and implementing biblical principles of environmental stewardship in private and public life. Such projects may never make the national evening news, but they are important avenues for Christians to work together and with others to change the world around them. The Christian community must stop being a culture in retreat. In these and many other ways, it must have a great enough love for God's people and God's world, and a great enough confidence in God, to risk involvement and make an impact.

The Church's Response

Much of this book has stressed biblical views and perspectives on the environment around us. In what ways should the church respond to the environmental problems of our time?

Balance and emphasis must have high priority in every church education program. Environmental topics should not lay claim to more time and effort than is due them simply because of the secular emphasis of the present age. However, in recent years there has been a dearth of sermons and Sunday-school studies on environmental themes, even though they are an integral part of the biblical message. In the past this may have been due to a lack of resources, but there is a growing amount of material on environmental topics in Christian perspective.[2] You can fulfill part of your responsibility to care for God's creation by asking your teacher or Sunday-school superintendent how much emphasis is given to environmental topics in the course of a church year. An adult Bible study on the biblical themes this book has detailed may be the very place to begin.

But such activity should not be restricted to adults. Youth groups need money, and there are better ways to earn it than washing cars. Recycling materials like newspapers, glass and aluminum can provide income as well. Youth can help local residents construct compost containers for using grass clippings and leaves as next year's mulch. Younger children can have activities and accomplishments directed toward conserving energy in the church, home and school. Service projects in the community can have environmental dimension and impact, like building trails at local preserves and developing nature centers and educational displays for next summer's church camp.

The preaching ministry of the church also has the opportunity, as well as the biblical responsibility, to emphasize a biblical view of creation in worship and instruction. A key to this is the enthusiastic acceptance by pastoral staff of the importance and relevance of revealing God as Creator and Sustainer, as well as our responsibility to care for God's world. Sermons can be developed around these themes, but even more important will be the attitude, perspective, commitment and modeling that come from pastors to congregations on the environmental problems of our world.

Finally, the church must enjoy worship and fellowship in God-made settings. This might occur in a local park or a camp. If it cannot be done by the entire church at once, it can begin with the individual classes and age groups within the larger church.

Church architecture should reflect the Creator's handiwork in the context of human responsibility for the creation. Just as church steeples and cathedral spires of past and present generations point heavenward, worship centers of today and tomorrow should feature open vistas of trees and clouds. Internal space should be aesthetically balanced with a rich diversity of living plants and of paintings and tapestries that reflect God's goodness in creation. Building design and materials should convey an understanding of energy conservation, with outdoor landscaping integrated into the overall design.[3]

Yet the church manages more than buildings. It is often a large property holder, both at the local level and through its denominations. We must model ecological responsibility on our grounds as well as our buildings. We can do this through our treatment of soil and water, our management of plant and animal resources at church camps, and our dedication to making all our properties places filled with beauty and life.

From Local to Global

From its origin, the church of Jesus Christ has engaged in missions, sending out believers to preach and teach the gospel to those in other lands. In our present day this work continues, albeit with changes in methods, technologies and strategies. Today many mission and development organizations emphasize a multidimensional ministry to meet spiritual, physical and economic need, especially for the poor in developing countries.[4] In such situations, the environmentally sensitive Christian worker needs to live with and learn from native people. It takes time and patience to understand the depth of local tradition and cultural heritage. The best approach is to encourage and support local efforts, and only gradually suggest some appropriate technological improvements. Health practices may be appalling to expatriates raised in a health-conscious Western environment, but changes in sanitation and cleanliness must proceed slowly and be carefully explained before others will be motivated to adopt them.

The population in many countries today, like Bangladesh and Kenya, is beyond the country's ability to support them. In countries like Uganda the AIDS virus is spreading rapidly. Parasitic infections remain widespread in tropical countries, and the advances of medical science in immunization, antibiotics and birth control have made only slight improvements in many countries that need them most.

So the time has come for the role of missions to expand. In addition to hospitals and medical care, evangelism and church planting, the establishment of Bible schools and seminaries, people of developing countries need other kinds of assistance too. Issues of population growth and economics confront people simultaneously. Developing countries can never attain healthy living standards without control of population growth—not through abortion but through caring counselors who can offer constructive advice and methods of family planning and birth control. Standards of living must improve to the point that elderly people can be cared for in other ways than by having large families. The development of small industry and improved agricultural methods for small farmers are steps in the right direction. In many countries such changes can only be preceded by land reform. Where the majority of land is owned by a small minority of the people, there can be little hope for justice.

In recent years some missionary statesmen have claimed that evangelism is fighting a losing battle and can never ultimately win because national populations grow faster than church memberships every year in many countries around the world. But a many-pronged strategy like that suggested above may help reverse this trend.

Environmental and human problems are closely connected. And like politics, all environmental consequences are ultimately local, experienced by one life, one family and one community at a time. They can be solved only by an integrated approach. The need of the hour is for the individual, the family and the church to extend their good work. One cannot remain complacent when oppression, poverty, disease and violence still consume so much of the world. Compassion is the act of love, working in the aftermath of flood, drought, famine, earthquake or any environmental catastrophe. These and other disasters affect not only human beings, but thousands of other creatures which God created and called good. We demonstrate God's love when we extend that compassion to them. We dare not cling to a faith that is personally exciting but socially irrelevant, lest we hear the judgment of Amos on us: "Away with the noise of your songs! I will not listen to the music of your harps. But let justice roll on like a river, righteousness like a never-failing stream!" (Amos 5:23-24).

Ethics, the Environment and Public Policy

To this point we have been making the assumption that the Christian's response to the environmental crisis consists primarily of personal choices and social cooperation. But it would be naive and mistaken to think that a sinful world will ever be without the need for reform on a larger scale. Environmental causes are no exception. To every issue the church and the Christian bring not only a redemptive role of healing but also a prophetic call to repentance. We illustrate that need for prophetic witness now in the retelling of some recent environmental events.

The Mumma-Mintzmyer hearings. On September 24, 1991, John Mumma, former forester of the U.S. Forest Service's Northern Region, testified before the Congressional Subcommittee on Civil Service in Washington, D.C. Lorraine Mintzmyer, former director of the National Park Service's Rocky Mountain Region, testified in the same subcommittee hearing. Both stated that they were being forcibly reassigned because of political pressure coming from outside their agencies.

Mumma claimed that this pressure was exerted because he did not meet timber harvest quotas in his region. Mumma, who had been described by some environmental groups as a reformer, said that description was inaccurate. He told the subcommittee, "All I tried to do was perform my job as a civil servant and to carry out the policies of the executive branch in accordance with federal law."[5] Mumma stated that he had failed to meet timber quotas "only because to do so would have required me to violate federal law," including the National Environmental Policy Act (NEPA), the National Forest Management Act and the Endangered Species Act.[6]

Mintzmyer stated that her reassignment came in response to her role in developing a scientifically based management document for the Greater Yellowstone Ecosystem; after it was rewritten under political pressure, she refused to tell the public that the revision was scientifically based.[7] The document she prepared was the Greater Yellowstone Vision Document, which, she claimed, angered Republican appointees in the Department of Interior and the White House. When the Vision Document had been almost completely rewritten and all of its major policy decisions revised, or even reversed, under political pressure, Mintzmyer resisted. "Stating that the vision document as it presently stands," Mintzmyer told the subcommittee, "is the result of efforts by the Park Service or the Forest Service, based on scientific considerations and the professional opinions of those agencies is, in my opinion, not accurate."[8]

Supervisors, political appointees and elected officials implicated in the Mumma-Mintzmyer testimony denied that political pressure played any role in their removals and reassignments. But such reassignments did occur coincident with the production of documents and the implementation of decisions that angered traditional Western commodity interests. Circumstances make the testimony of Mumma and Mintzmyer, who had nothing to gain from testifying and everything to lose, extremely believable.

Further investigation also tended to corroborate their testimony. On January 8, 1993, the Associated Press reported that the staff report of the House Civil Service Subcommittee concluded that Interior Department officials conspired with timber, livestock and mining interests to gut an environmental blueprint (the so-called Vision Document) for Yellowstone National Park and its surrounding national forests. The report claimed that Interior Department officials retaliated against both Mintzmyer and Mumma, cochairs of the team that produced the Vision Document, and that the officials engaged in an underhanded, politically motivated operation to destroy the draft document because it was unacceptable to powerful commodity interests. The subcommittee's chief counsel, Kimberly L. Japinga, said the report had not yet been officially approved by the subcommittee and may not represent the views of all the subcommittee's members. Senator Alan Simpson (Republican, Wyoming) called the report "absurd and stupid," and Interior Department officials called it a "witch hunt" and "political gamesmanship." So the controversy continues.

The testimonies of Mumma and Mintzmyer reflect different but related issues in environmental ethics. In the first case, Mumma describes a situation in which a management objective can be achieved only by breaking environmental law. In the second, Mintzmyer testifies that a federal agency, the National Park Service, is asked to deliberately misrepresent the source and nature of information contained in a critical management document, a document intended to form the basis of future management of the nation's oldest and most popular national park and the seven national forests adjoining it. What is unusual in each case is the extremely high level of the people making the accusations. As a regional forester, Mumma reported directly to Forest Service Chief Dale Robertson. As a regional director of the Park Service, Mintzmyer reported directly to National Park Service Director James Ridenour. People so advanced and so entrenched in agency bureaucracies are not normally notorious troublemakers. And they do not value their careers lightly. The fact that senior-level executives were willing to resist agency directives to the degree that they did should concern us and lead us to probe more deeply into how our natural resources are actually being managed.

The cases of Mintzmyer and Mumma are unusual because of the high level of their positions. But many government employees at lower levels are also routinely reassigned, transferred or dismissed when their personal determination to uphold environmental law is considered politically inappropriate. In the *Audubon* article "When a Whistle Blows in the Forest," Paul Schneider documents notable cases within the Forest Service in which individual careers were effectively terminated for such activities as protecting archaeological sites, finding endangered plants in proposed timber-sale areas or reducing overall timber harvest quotas to benefit wildlife or watersheds.

Even more disturbing than the individual incidents documented by Schneider are the perceptions of the Forest Service's priorities among its own employees. When asked, in an agency survey, to choose from among twenty attributes they felt would be most rewarded by the Forest Service, agency personnel ranked loyalty to the Forest Service, meeting targets and promoting a good image of the Forest Service as the three most rewarded worker attributes. The three attributes considered least rewarded were a sense of care for future generations, the preservation of healthy ecosystems and a strong professional identity.[9]

A deeper crisis. Forest Service workers are not some sort of alien nation, but a subset of the American population at large. As such, they both represent that population's values and are influenced by them. As public values shift away from the traditional commodity interests of timber, minerals and grazing and toward noncommodity interests of wildlife, recreation and aesthetics, tension grows between management directives that benefit commodities and environmental laws designed to protect long-term ecosystem health. That tension is being increasingly reflected in the growth of organizations within the Forest Service itself, like Forest Service Employees for Environmental Ethics and Inner Voices—groups that advocate greater attention to long-term environmental stewardship.

There have been other recent examples of environmental lawbreaking in Forest Service management activities. In 1985 and 1990, timber was logged in two wilderness areas in Oregon, despite a ban on such activities in the Wilderness Act of 1964. In the management of wilderness itself, the House Committee on Appropriations was distressed to discover that only 63 percent of the Forest Service's appropriated budget for wilderness was actually spent on wilderness management between 1988 and 1990, and only a little over half of the funds provided for wilderness management in fiscal year 1990 were actually used for wilderness.

The Forest Service generates much of its own revenue from timber sales, but the timber sales it prepares are not always cost-effective. Michael Lipske reported in 1990 that according to Congressional estimates the Forest Service lost as much as $350 million in its Tongas National Forest timber sales in Alaska.[10] Resource economist Randall O'Toole estimated that timber sales on the seven forests surrounding Yellowstone National Park lost $12.2 million in 1988.[11] Yet cost-ineffective timber sales continue, notes O'Toole, because "timber sales, whether they make or lose money, produce many jobs—and therefore votes—in a state or congressional district."[12] This situation is aggravated by the fact that, legally, forest managers may keep an unlimited share of gross timber receipts for forest management activities in the timber sale area and are under no obligation to return an equal share to the U.S. Treasury, the source of funds for timber sale arrangement and preparation.[13] This situation has resulted in such absurd activities as logging forests in critical grizzly-bear habitat to raise funds to improve grizzly-bear habitat—a situation that actually occurred in the Gallatin National Forest in Montana.[14]

Another major U.S. federal agency, the National Park Service, has come under increasing criticism for the long-term loss of mammal species in national parks, for spending less than 1 percent of a billion-dollar budget on basic research and for managing the parks under the guidance of a core of nonprofessional police officers, the park rangers, rather than professional scientists.[15]

A Path to Reform

In the wake of the scandal surrounding the Mintzmyer-Mumma hearings, journalist Ed Marston, editor of the Western environmental newspaper *High Country News,* wrote an editorial entitled "Will the Bush Administration Choose Reform?" The last word in the title was portentous, because nothing short of reform is needed in American resource management agencies to make them effective in accomplishing their mission. As the true picture of how resources are being managed in this country becomes clearer, it is apparent that the word *corruption* would not be misapplied in many cases. As Marston puts it, "The West's commodity producers—unwilling or unable to adapt to the nation's new land ethic—appear determined to continue their economic activities outside the law. They have chosen outlaw status."[16]

The effect of such behavior is to dissolve values into power. But power exercised in contradiction to value is not legitimate power; it is coercion. In the absence of a normative public ethic, we have arrived at the situation in which politics, as Alasdair MacIntyre put it, "becomes civil war carried on by other means."[17]

Evil in Society: The Christian's Political Response

Theologians distinguish between two types of evil—personal and structural.[18] Personal evil, the problem of individual sin and moral choice, is the subject of many sermons. The Christian's response to personal evil is a change in personal behavior. It requires repentance, restitution and subsequent consecration to God. As Paul told the church at Ephesus, "Let him who steals steal no longer, but rather let him labor, performing with his own hands what is good, in order that he may have

156 _____ *Redeeming Creation*

something to share with him who has need" (Ephesians 4:28 NASB).

But evil in a fallen world can reach beyond personal levels and demand more than personal responses. Evil can come to be incorporated, and even rewarded, in the operation of a system or organization. Evil at the structural level cannot be effectively thwarted by remedies at the personal level. It is the system itself that must be changed.

There are many who have proposed changes. Randall O'Toole, seeing the structural evils of the Forest Service as primarily economic, proposes an economic solution: charge fees for recreational use of national forest lands, and then allow managers to keep the funds generated from such fees for use in their forests or districts.[19] This plan has many merits, but standing alone it is incomplete. O'Toole's answer equates maximum revenue with moral excellence. And neither the Mumma nor the Mintzmyer case was based on solely economic motives.

Alston Chase, one of the most widely published critics of the National Park Service, proposes sweeping changes in the National Park Service budget and its employee evaluation system, along with an increasing role for external review.[20] Chase's proposals, if implemented, would have many beneficial effects. But they do not address the deeper questions of the moral legitimacy of Park Service policies.

Not only the economic and management structure but the entire legal structure of American property law must change if there is to be real reform in resource management. Joseph Sax, professor at the University of California-Berkeley School of Law, states that "a fundamental purpose of the traditional system of property law has been to destroy the functioning of natural resource systems."[21] And Sax is right, for enclosure and exclusion, the foundation of private property laws, water rights laws, homesteading laws, swamp drainage laws and multitudes of other laws are essential to private control of land productivity, but anathema to the ecological health of natural systems and communities. Saying this does not imply that private property is evil or illegitimate, but private-property law often miscarries when it is applied to public lands and public resources.

Traditional private-property law, upon which long-standing resource commodity interests on public lands are based, now runs into increasing conflict with more recent legislation aimed at protecting ecosystem health in the public interest. When such laws were either not in existence or not enforced, we began to develop, and sometimes did develop, what Garrett Hardin described as "the Tragedy of the Commons." Each individual, acting as a private entity on public lands, wants to maximize his profit. If he should add one more cow, cut one more tree or mine one more ton of ore, he experiences, for his effort, both a negative and a positive effect. Negatively, he degrades the resource, his capital, on which he depends. Positively, he receives another increment of profit. But as Hardin points out, the negative and positive outcomes are not equal. The negative is shared (spread) among all the resource users, and all share the cost. The positive (one more cow, tree or ton of ore) is the individual owner's, and his alone. So each one, quite rationally, tries to increase profit without limit in a world that is in fact very limited. The inevitable outcome is the ruination of the resource and the economies that depend on it.[22]

We are seeing the truth of this principle played in ten thousand times ten thousand scenarios in the economies of the rural West, where the problem is blamed on spotted owls, insensitive bureaucrats or too much government. But the truth is that resource-based economies cannot expand without limit in a limited world. And recent environmentally protective legislation such as the National Environmental Policy Act and the Endangered Species Act is forced to confront this traditional assumption. As this recent legislation erodes the legal power of grazing, mining, logging and other commodity interests, such interests must resort more and more to the use of direct political power, with which they are still amply supplied. But now, in contrast to the past, this power must more and more often be used outside the law. That is, it must be used illegally.

Whenever any group uses power without legal foundation, the result is not democracy but a dictatorship of politically powerful outlaws. The outcome of using power in this way is the corruption of the entire natural resource management system and the illegal degradation of legally protected resources. Even in the United States, traditionally the most lawful of countries, we are witnessing both. The most obvious manifestation has been the growth of the so-called Wise-Use movement in the United States. Groups within this movement, while claiming grassroots support, are often funded by resource-exploiting companies and are not averse to using tactics of intimidation and violence against environmentalists.[23]

Reform is needed in the structures of management and the structures of law. But by themselves the reforms generated in these areas would still be incomplete. A further, and greater, need is the development and provision of an environmental ethic by which both individuals and agencies are judged. And until that ethic is well formulated and well articulated, neither personal nor structural evil in natural resource management can be effectively attacked.

Aldo Leopold foresaw the dangers of an inadequate basis of environmental ethics and warned what would happen to those who tried to build a comprehensive program of conservation upon them.

No important change in ethics was ever accomplished without an internal change in our intellectual emphasis, loyalties, affections, and convictions. The proof that conservation has not yet touched these foundations of conduct lies in the fact that philosophy and religion have not yet heard of it. In our attempt to make conservation easy we have made it trivial. When the logic of history hungers for bread and we hand out a stone, we are at pains to explain how much the stone resembles bread.[24]

But as has been described earlier, Leopold's own attempt to develop a meaningful environmental ethic also failed, precisely because he did not follow his own advice and neglected to connect his own ethic with the roots of philosophy or religion. No ethic was ever established simply by proclamation or eloquence. Ethics become meaningful only when they are connected with lasting sources of value and tradition.

Because of this neglect of ethical foundations, the present environmental movement races toward a crisis of irresolvable value conflicts, a crisis that can result only in further degradation of God's good creation. It is to this internal crisis of environmental ethics, even more than the external crisis of environmental degradation, that the Christian community, the church, must respond. The church has the most resources to offer for meeting this great need. But it is this need that will demand the greatest and most costly sacrifice.

The Christian Church and Prophetic Witness
Theologian Carl F. H. Henry has said, "It is only as each Christian generation permeates its environment with biblical moral sensitivities

that unregenerate society is restrained from acting on its deep-seated prejudices and is encouraged to judge itself by Christian ideals—even when it is unwilling to embrace those ideals as an explicit intellectual commitment."[25] In the cases of Mumma and Mintzmyer, and in the cases of hundreds of other government employees at lower levels, we come to see all too clearly what those "deep-seated prejudices" really are and how they express themselves. They are the prejudices of self-interest. And they are comfortably at home in even our noblest national effort, the protection of the environment. The expression of such prejudices is simple and direct: If the law is contrary to your desires, break it. If the truth does not support your position, lie. And if others stand in your way, have them removed.

We are left at this point with a sobering realization. The most basic reform of all, and one that only the church can provide, is the provision of a meaningful environmental ethic by which both individuals and agencies are judged and which has the strength to bring personal evil to repentance and structural evil to reform. Both the political and the physical environment have seen an endless parade of attempts to achieve ethics by proclamation, ethics that have had no roots in anything but their author's last journal article. No ethic in American resource management can hope to successfully and persistently influence the public behavior of ordinary people unless it is informed by biblical values.

The response of the Christian community in providing a new ethic, a new standard, by which resource management as well as resource managers can be judged, must take place at three levels. The first is to produce a new kind of individual, the steward, who has self-consciously internalized and learned to practice a biblical ethic of resource management and to apply such an ethic within a technical, professional discipline. And if it sounds paradoxical that the first response of a community should sound so individualistic, one can only reply that the church as a community has been doing exactly that for centuries. By Christ's power it has not merely been changing nasty people into nice people, but natural humans into "new creations" (2 Corinthians 5:17). And even if we might be tempted to wish for something less radical, the truth is that nothing else will do.

We are pleased to see the publication of *An Evangelical Declaration on the Care of Creation,* a document produced by the Evangelical Environmental Network (EEN) and signed by more than 120 of North America's most prominent and influential Christian leaders. The EEN was formed as an offshoot of Ron Sider's organization Evangelicals for Social Action, and it aspires to be a continuing influence toward a biblically based environmental ethic in the days ahead. The EEN's initial statement is an excellent beginning in defining both the theology for the care of God's creation and the needed response of the evangelical community. But words are valuable only if they rest on the integrity of those committed to act. And the Christian community must move beyond statements and manifestos to deeds that produce real solutions. The ongoing work of the Society of the Green Cross, mentioned earlier, provides hope for a growing and lasting witness of evangelical Christians on environmental issues.

To reach this point, the church must, second, make a corporate commitment of training its stewards through graduate degree programs in its colleges. And in those colleges it must provide not merely education but also the supportive community that will give plausibility to the biblical ethics of stewardship.

Third, these stewards must join with the church in public involvement and debate over resource management issues and decisions in order to make biblical principles part of the public discussion of resource values, the basis on which management decisions are made and the criteria by which right and wrong conduct in resource management is judged. This is the church's social response, the interface between itself and society on this critical issue.

The very idea of biblical principles' being involved in public debate will seem shocking to some and unacceptable to others, but it is nonetheless necessary. We recoil from the idea because even as Christians, we have accepted the secularist's premise that religion may be personally enthralling but is socially irrelevant—that it is some sort of private vice, like pornography, to be practiced in one's closet. We, the authors, utterly reject these premises and stand with the witness of history, which has seen countless Christian women and men treat faith not as a private perversion but as a moral ideal that led them—indeed compelled them—to speak and act publicly against evil, and to do so on biblical principles. In the final chapter we examine more fully the strategies of these three responses and the costs that they entail.

Questions for Thought and Discussion

1. What is the difference between personal and structural evil? What kinds of environmental problems must be addressed at the personal level? What kinds must be addressed at the structural level?

2. Name one specific action you could take in each of the following areas to make yourself a more effective steward toward God's creation: (1) informed study, (2) deliberate contact, (3) sacrificial concern.

3. How do events described in this chapter support the idea that a stronger and more biblically informed ethical basis is needed in managing natural resources?

4. In what ways could you influence your own church to corporately express its faith in God as Creator and the world as his creation?

10
Ecology & the Christian Mind
A New Beginning

Who so hath his minde on taking, hath it no
more on what he has taken.
M O N T A I G N E [1]

CARL SAGAN, THE NOTED ASTRONOMER AND SPOKESMAN OF SCI-
ence, published a letter in the July 1990 issue of the *American
Journal of Physics* in which he called for a joint commitment by
"science and religion" to preserve and cherish the earth.[2] After briefly
reviewing some of the major environmental problems, Sagan wrote,
"We are close to committing—many would argue we are already committing—what in religious language is sometimes called Crimes against
Creation."[3]

Sagan continued, saying that our environmental problems require
"radical changes not only in public policy, but also in individual
behavior. The historical record makes clear that religious teaching,
example, and leadership are powerfully able to influence personal
conduct and commitment."[4] Speaking for the scientific community, he
concluded that as scientists "we understand that what is regarded as
sacred is more likely to be treated with care and respect. Our planetary
home should be so regarded."[5]

This letter was not the first such appeal by Sagan. The Global Forum
of Spiritual and Parliamentary Leaders on Human Survival, held in
Moscow in January 1990, attracted more than one thousand religious,
political and scientific leaders from eighty-three nations, including

United Nations Secretary General Javier Pérez de Cuellar, Nobel Peace Prize winner Elie Wiesel and Mikhail Gorbachev.[6] A joint religious-scientific initiative emerging from that meeting was a commitment for "preserving and cherishing the earth." The initiative was led by Carl Sagan. Other statements included the "Moscow Declaration," which called for a new "planetary perspective" to include "a spiritual and ethical basis for human activities on earth." And the forum's "Plan of Action" included many measures to raise public consciousness and concrete steps to reverse environmental destruction through "fundamental change in the attitudes and practices that have pushed our world to a perilous brink."[7]

It is worth pausing in this final chapter to consider the implications of such appeals, for they highlight the key issues that this book has tried to address. They force us to understand what makes an environmental ethic genuinely Christian and to perceive what lies ahead for the church in the coming environmental age. And in understanding them we are prepared to conclude what the previous chapter began, the response of the church and its people to the ecologic crisis.

Taking Our Bearings: Where We Have Been

Scientist René Dubos wrote,

> When first investigated, the cave floor of the Choukoutien cave, which had been occupied by *Homo erectus* 500,000 years ago, was littered with the charred bones of horses, sheep, pigs, buffalo, and deer. More recent prehistoric sites contain food residues which had been casually abandoned by the occupants over many generations, along with artifacts of stone, bone, ivory, or pottery. Such accumulations of products and objects are an essential source of documentation for the archaeologist. . . . But from another point of view . . . [they] can be regarded as the garbage of primitive humankind. They are the equivalents of beer cans, plastic junk, radios, bedsteads, and automobile carcasses that litter modern highways and settlements.[8]

In light of such data, it is not surprising that Dubos perceived that fatal flaw in his countryman French philosopher Jean-Jacques Rousseau's assessment of human nature and its relation to the environment. "Rousseau," wrote Dubos, "believed that human nature was intrinsically good until it was sullied by civilization. The fashionable view at present is that human nature was bad from the very beginning and civilization has only given wider ranges of expression to its fundamental bestiality."[9]

This "fashionable view" does not follow historian Lynn White Jr. in assigning the causes of our environmental crisis to a particular world-view, like Christianity, or to the civilization most influenced by it, medieval Europe.[10] Rather, Dubos and others understand that there is something fundamentally wrong with human nature itself. It is "bestial," to use Dubos's word. This fundamental depravity within human nature expresses itself in, among other things, a destructiveness toward the physical world. It is, at heart, an expression of the selfishness of humankind.

Jonathan Edwards, an eighteenth-century theologian, describes the cause:

> Immediately upon the fall, the mind of man shrank from its primitive greatness and expandedness, to an exceeding smallness and contractedness. . . . Before, his soul was under the government of the noble principle of divine love, whereby it was enlarged to the comprehensiveness of all his fellow creatures and their welfare. . . . [But] sin, like some powerful astringent, contracted his soul to the very small dimensions of selfishness, and God was forsaken, and man retired within himself, and became totally governed by narrow and selfish principles and feelings.[11]

It is amazing that Edwards should be able to describe so precisely and powerfully what modern environmental philosophers like Garrett Hardin can only puzzle over as a bizarre quirk of human societies—namely, that humans find selfishness more natural (and more profitable) than cooperation, with environmental destruction the logical result.[12]

While such behavior is not unique to American culture, it has always been very much at home in it. In colonial America, William Penn provided a positive example of good stewardship by prescribing that on his lands one acre of forest was to be left standing for every five that were cleared.[13] But George Washington expressed his embarrassment over more typical American farmers in a letter to Arthur Young, noting that the goal of such farmers was "not to make the most they can from the land, which is . . . cheap, but the most of the labor, which is dear;

the consequence of which has been, much ground has been scratched over and none cultivated or improved as it ought to have been."[14] In these perceptions of the father of our country, the words of Genesis are flung stinging back upon us: "The LORD God took the man and put him in the Garden of Eden to work it and take care of it" (2:15).

A Beginning: Right Thinking About Creator and Creation

Ethicist James Gustafson has summarized two basic ways of looking at the application of theology to social issues. One is to begin with some pressing moral and social question. When we have a clear view of the question, we can turn to the resources of theology and religious practice to establish the theological and religious "answer." The second is to begin with a more basic question: What do we know about God and his plans, and how do we know it? In Gustafson's own words, "What can we affirm . . . about God's purposes for life in the world? What beliefs about God pertain to the moral issues we face in time and place . . . of contemporary life?"[15] We think, with Gustafson, that the second approach is better. In fact, it is the use of the first approach that contributes to the weakness of much Christian writing about ecologic problems today.

Theologian J. I. Packer addresses this point powerfully in the final paragraph of his classic book *Knowing God:*

> From current Christian publications you might think that the most vital issue for any real or would-be Christian in the world today is church union, or social witness, or dialogue with other Christians and other faiths, or refuting this or that -ism, or developing a Christian philosophy and culture. . . . But our line of study makes the present day concentration on these things look like a gigantic conspiracy of misdirection.[16]

Packer goes on to make clear that this is not necessarily the case. The issues are real and must be dealt with. But the true priority of every human being is to know God in Christ. From that perspective, and to avoid making this book part of that "conspiracy of misdirection," we must summarize the issues of this book from a larger perspective.

God the Creator

We have already seen (in chapter two) that God chose to reveal himself to us first as the Creator. This choice is neither accidental nor inappropriate, but the emphasis on God as Creator is sadly neglected in the teachings of the church. In an effort to avoid conflict (some real, some imagined) with science, the church has soft-pedaled (sometimes backpedaled) the truth that the cosmos and all it contains is God's creation.

The idea of creation is one of the single most powerful ideas to have ever arisen in Western culture.[17] Indeed, our culture's present loss of this idea has contributed to its increasing loss of optimism and of reality. Creation defines our place in the cosmos and our position before the living God, our Creator, just as it also defines our common bonds with other creatures and our special responsibilities to them. *Creator* and *creation* are words and concepts the church must reclaim if it is to successfully lead people to know God and his world as they really are, and not merely as we might think them to be. To know God as Creator is to know that he is preexistent and self-existent, that he is transcendent (not the same as what he has made), that he is immanent (present with us) and that he is free, creating for his own purposes, not ours.

It is only in knowing God as Creator and the universe as his creation that we can begin to contemplate the immensity of the person and work and purposes of God. And in the present age, when people are all too ready to imagine God as some sort of celestial bellhop assigned to their own room service, no Christian can get along without the knowledge of God as Creator. In fact, it is essential if one is to presume to know God at all.

The Celebration of Creation
Because our culture has lost its belief in God the Creator, it has also lost any spontaneous joy in the works of creation. Despite creation's grandeur and beauty, intelligent people can have difficulty finding lasting joy in physical objects which they believe to be simply the outcome of time plus the impersonal plus chance. The church, in its attempt to appear sophisticated and mimic society's "objectivity," also has robbed God's people of such joy. Such an approach to the works of creation is not in fact sophistication, but stupidity. This callous reserve is nothing but a concealed form of pride. The Bible teaches the believer to say with the psalmist, "How many are your works, O LORD! In wisdom you made them all" (Psalm 104:24). It teaches us to

find joy in the wonder of rock badgers and wild goats, in lions and storks, in moon and sun and stars (Psalm 104). The Bible even teaches the believer to find joy (with reverence) in the power and destruction of a thunderstorm (Psalm 29). The Bible does this not because these things prove God's existence (as though the Creator depended on his creatures for this) but because they are simply *his*. They are his creatures and his works, and they exist for his pleasure. To understand this is to begin to understand the joy of the psalmist and say with him, "May the glory of the LORD endure forever" (Psalm 104:31).

To know God as Creator we must celebrate his creation. This means that it is hypocrisy for a Christian to willfully live separated from God's creation and the joy of it. Just as Christians cannot get along without knowing God as Creator, so knowing the joy of God's creation (through informed study, deliberate contact and sacrificial concern) is an essential element to the joy of Christian life.

The Obedience of Ruling and Subduing

As Christians cannot be indifferent to knowing God as Creator, or to the joy of celebrating his creation, so they cannot be indifferent to the needs of creation, especially when these needs express themselves as the ecological crises of the modern world. Because ruling, in the kingdom of God, is to be expressed by service to those ruled (as we noted in chapter six) and by the command to cultivate and keep (Genesis 2:15), management and preservation combine in the concept of stewardship. While the stewardship of creation is a professional calling for some Christians who serve as scientists and resource managers, it must be the avocation of every Christian. Involvement in the care of creation, both corporately and individually, on issues of both worldwide concern and local significance, represents every Christian's appropriate obedience to the imperative of Genesis 1:28.

Intelligent, active involvement with creation has not been and will not be unique to the Christian community. Indeed, the church has lagged far behind other groups in recognizing the rightness of caring for creation. What is unique to Christians is the ability to act without internal conflict and intellectual contradiction. To have a reason to act, Christians do not need to claim (falsely) a complete identity with the earth and its creatures. On the other hand, Christians do not need to claim (inconsistently) to be merely plain citizens of nature and then assume that they should make life-and-death decisions about creation's welfare. Stewardship of creation is demanded by something greater than the survivalist mentality inherent in many modern environmental appeals. It is demanded by humanity's unique position in creation as the image of God. So we are exalted to act as God's servants and representatives to other creatures in this present age. But we are also, in the same acts of stewardship, humbled, for we also are creatures, and we stand accountable before God for the outcomes of any action we take.[18]

The Vision of Christian Ecological Education

In northern lower Michigan near the small town of Mancelona, there is a place called the Au Sable Institute of Environmental Studies. Serving as a field campus for a consortium of Christian colleges and universities throughout the United States and Canada, Au Sable, in the words of its official bulletin (1993), offers

> programs of study for college students, research projects and forums, environmental education for local school children, and information services for churches, denominations and the wider world community. Supported by surrounding forests, wetlands, lakes and rivers, participants take courses, engage in scholarship, gain field experience, confer, and develop practical tools for environmental stewardship in programs that take seriously both science and theology.[19]

Au Sable is, to our knowledge, the only institution of its kind. Since its inception in 1982, it has trained hundreds of students in the professional and practical application of Christian resource stewardship.

Au Sable is one example of the living reality of the first strategy described at the end of chapter nine: it is an institution dedicated to the production of an entirely new kind of resource manager, the steward. To understand why the production of this kind of individual is so critical, we must contrast the steward with a type of professional common in resource management today: the careerist.

The Careerist Versus the Steward

It is fair to say that most people who enter the field of resource management choose their career with high motives. They intend to protect the environment, maintain ecosystems, save endangered species and educate the public. Unfortunately, their instructors have taught them that following these ideals is not going to cost anything to anybody—least of all themselves and their own advancement. They are the ones Leopold spoke of when he said, "In our attempt to make conservation easy, we have made it trivial."

Praise and advancement will be attractively offered and will often come in response to right actions. But as years go by and promotions and earnings accumulate, a strange and sinister thing begins to happen. The career itself, with its attendant praise and advancement, begins to become more important than the ideals for which it was chosen. And then, almost unconsciously, the person begins to protect not the resource but the career. In time the steward becomes a careerist. And the careerist can always be persuaded, with the right combinations of reason and reward, to rationalize, support and, ultimately, initiate decisions that do God's creatures and God's creation much harm, but that do a career great good.

So evil achieves one of its greatest, most subtle and yet most complete triumphs. It persuades men and women who are not yet very bad people to do very bad things. And such evil, once entrenched, becomes a part of the very fabric of organizations, governments and societies.

Against the role of the careerist, God presents to human beings the role of the steward, whose tasks are to cultivate, keep and name (know and understand) to the glory of God and the good of creation and creatures. To this steward, made in his image, God has given the authority to rule and subdue. And by word and example God defines *authority* and *rulership* as service to one's subjects, placing their needs ahead of one's own.

The church must make clear the contrast between the careerist and the steward and say that the first path is wrong and the second is right. Only in this way are the deep-seated prejudices of self-interest, present even in the noble effort of saving the environment, fully exposed and restrained from controlling that effort and rendering it worthless.

Christians and Higher Education

For Christian higher education, the question of the future is, Will the Au Sable Institute remain the only one of its kind? In his classic science-fiction Foundation trilogy Isaac Asimov tells of the decline of a decadent galactic empire. Foreseeing its collapse and the centuries of chaos that will follow, one of the empire's most brilliant scientists secretly establishes two new communities, the Foundation Colonies, in different parts of the galaxy. Their ultimate purpose is to replace the decadent empire as a new and better source of order, peace and enlightenment in the galaxy. Asimov's trilogy is the story of the struggle of these colonies. In the same way, environmental ethics based on inadequate value systems must ultimately lead to irresolvable conflicts and crises and, in time, moral chaos. This outcome is inevitable. What is still in doubt is whether the Christian educational community will recognize the coming collapse of such ethical systems and seize the opportunity to become the new foundation.

The church itself must recognize that it is the community that must teach, train and produce stewards. No one else is going to do it. We must build people of personal integrity who actually are stewards and function professionally as stewards, not just make judgments about who is one and who is not. To do this the church must recognize that since we want to prepare people to combat corporate structural evil, we must make the training of such people a corporate mission. Specifically, this requires the church to do three things.

First, we must state that the work of the steward for God's creation is a mission in God's service, and that it therefore receives, unhesitatingly, the joyful support and prayer of the church.

Second, we must commit our educational resources—our colleges—to train stewards capable of working professionally in resource management. The beginning of this recognition will be the establishment of programs in graduate environmental education at Christian colleges and institutes. At present many Christian colleges are giving degrees in biology to people who are both unequipped and unprepared to function as professional ecologists; the assumption is that state universities will remedy this deficiency in their graduate schools. What Christian colleges must do instead is to strengthen their undergraduate programs in biology and ecology and initiate graduate programs in resource management.

The present practice of sending the best and brightest students to complete their graduate education at state universities has done both

Christian education and environmental stewardship much harm. While interchange and training within the entire scientific community are always valuable, indoctrination in a secular system of values is always harmful. Its outcome is a class of people whom C. S. Lewis rightly called "men without chests."[20] Many products of such training have been taught to believe in a dichotomy of two worlds, a world of fact without a trace of value and a world of values without one trace of truth or falsehood.[21]

This dualism of facts and values manifests itself in a very real way in the debate over appropriate uses of public lands. With no normative ethic to serve as a guide, the resource manager must treat every value judgment simply as the assertion of a private interest. Thus the manager then becomes not a steward applying moral excellence to the decisions and dilemmas of resource management but merely a manipulator of public input whose only job is to appease various interest groups.

The more our technological power grows, the more deadly the inadequacy of secular education becomes. The greater the skill acquired to remake the earth, the greater the training that *must be* required to teach skills and values of care and responsibility. As Wendell Berry has said, "To think or act without cultural value, and the restraints invariably implicit in cultural value, is simply to wait upon force."[22]

The church must recognize that in training stewards, our colleges are more than schools. They are communities. As such, they must provide the personal support and plausibility structure for an entirely new approach to resource management. Such an approach will appear deviant and threatening to the resource management establishment, of which the state universities are a part. The plausibility of ideas depends on the social support they receive.[23] And as sociologist Peter Berger rightly perceives, we obtain our notions of the world from others. These notions continue to be plausible to us to the extent that they continue to be affirmed by others with whom we relate.

We must consider secularism a false and inadequate education for stewards if we really believe that there is more to stewardship than careerism, and if we really believe that the present crisis in environmental ethics will not be solved merely by technical skill but by the production of a new kind of person who manages resources in an entirely new way. And if we do not believe that, any discussion of the church's role in environmental ethics and policy is pointless.

Though the failure of Christian colleges to provide graduate training in environmental sciences has been due in part to a lack of resources, it is primarily a lack of vision that has kept those colleges and their constituencies from seeking the resources necessary to begin. The work cannot be put off any longer. The Christian educational community must make the commitment to provide professional graduate-level training in resource sciences if it hopes to lay a new foundation of environmental ethics and management.

If Christian colleges fail to produce individuals in whom factual knowledge, technical skill and professional credentials are wedded to moral conviction, the Christian community has no hope of influencing the outcome of the environmental crisis. Thus far, one of the most important reasons that the Christian community does not significantly affect public environmental policy is that its educational system has not developed the graduate schools necessary to produce public policy makers.

Third, the church and its scholars must actively and prayerfully support Christian women and men who are now engaged in graduate degree programs in secular universities. Scholarships, fellowships, conferences, classes, Bible studies and personal encouragement from established Christian scholars in many fields can help those now engaged in graduate study to understand their discipline within biblical perspectives and to devote their scholarship to the service of God.

The Church and Society: Political Involvement and Environmental Ethics

In his classic work *Rich Christians in an Age of Hunger,* Ron Sider was one of the first evangelical scholars in the second half of the twentieth century to insist that the church must act corporately and politically if it is to attack structural evil.[24] Sider's work clarifies an important principle. To make the stewards it produces effective, the church must state publicly and corporately what a biblical ethic of environmental stewardship is and then make such an ethic part of the public discussion of environmental values and decisions. This is an appropriate prophetic witness for the church, carrying both a proclamation of biblical truth and a judgment against evil.

In the United States many federal environmental laws, such as the National Environmental Policy Act (NEPA), require federal agencies to solicit public comment and review. This comment and review must be thoughtful and intelligent if it is to receive serious consideration, but it can address basic questions of value and ethics. For example, it is common for Native American tribal governments to make specific recommendations to agencies like the Forest Service during the NEPA process about specific land-use plans and management practices—recommendations based on the tribe's religious beliefs and its traditions of sacred sites. The Forest Service takes such comments seriously and will modify its actions and policies if the arguments are persuasive.

One would get the impression that the church does not take its own religious beliefs as seriously as these tribal governments take theirs, for we have yet to see an individual church or denomination enter this public process to present valid biblical concepts about stewardship which would have far-reaching effects on natural resource management and policy in the United States.

Perhaps the reason the church does not do this is that as we pointed out in the previous chapter, we as its members have come to believe the propaganda of our critics—that Christian faith may be personally enthralling but is socially irrelevant. If there is any hope of reform for natural resource management in the United States, the church must realize that our present privatization of faith is an unacceptable, introspective pietism that must be abandoned. Faith is always deeply personal, but it must never be allowed to remain merely personal. As Richard John Neuhaus states in *The Naked Public Square,* the American public square of discussion and debate on public policy cannot remain naked of Christian meaning and purpose indefinitely. If it does not come to be clothed with meaning beyond mere social pragmatism, it will eventually cease to function altogether, or it will be clothed with spiritual but non-Christian meaning from other sources.[25] And then, as Jesus said, the last condition will be worse than the first.

In publicly presenting biblical ideas as part of the discussion on resource management, the church also must present the standard for ethics in resource management (and for resource managers). Such presentation will immediately reveal the need for reform. The church should not be troubled by its critics who will ask, "Where have you been on this issue all these years?" or who will point out that the church does not have perfect moral or professional credentials on environmental issues (or anything else, for that matter). Roy Enquist replies best when he writes, "Perfectionism is no more appropriate in the shaping of social teaching than in any other church activity. It is the unwillingness to attempt to speak a concrete Word of the Lord in our time of moral squalor, rather than the inability to do it perfectly, that renders the community's witness suspect."[26]

As the need for reform is progressively revealed by the church's witness and involvement, the church must state what the path to reform is, in both agencies and individuals, and how it can be followed. It is impossible to do this simply by setting up a denominational task force, writing a position statement and then going on to something else. To be an effective prophetic witness, the church must have a standing body of individuals actively involved with ongoing resource management decisions, persistently presenting, in every public forum, biblical positions and their relation to resource management actions. In this context, it is appropriate for Christians to act corporately across denominational lines by forming and joining environmental advocacy groups that are explicitly Christian, such as the Christian Environmental Association and the Society of the Green Cross. This is not to say that Christians should withdraw from groups that are not exclusively Christian. But it must be recognized that such groups usually do not, indeed cannot, address issues at the deepest ethical levels, nor can they provide the basis for reform at such levels.

The strategies the church must follow, both to provide a biblical ethic to society and to guide reform within resource management, require a costly commitment. They require recognition of the care of creation as a priority. They require public participation with unsympathetic and at times hostile audiences. They require investment of time and money. But for all that, they are, in the words of George MacDonald, something that is not to be more, nor less, nor other than done. There can be no lasting environmental ethic and no meaningful environmental reform without them.

Witness: The Proclamation
To know God as Creator is not an addendum of the Christian life but

an essential revelation of the character and person of God. Because it is an integral part of God's revelation to us, it likewise must be an integral part of our witness to humanity. In his book *The Gravedigger File* Os Guinness illustrates two aspects of Christian witness that make it believable. One is credibility, to state and defend what Christians believe and why they believe it. The other is plausibility, to make such belief "seem" true by the way Christians live, individually and together.[27] Careful preparation and diligent research can make our words *sound* true. But what personal characteristics in our own lives will make them *seem* true?

To make Christian witness as stewards plausible, our lives must reflect certain essential qualities. First, we must find and express genuine joy in the works of God's creation. This means that we must seek them out, visit them, value them and appreciate them, wherever we live. We must not live out all our days in environments entirely of our own making. Though amusement parks like Disney World are remarkable human achievements, they pale next to what God has done in creation. Sadly, we often seek and experience more of the former than the latter.

Second, we must be careful and humble in the ways we use creation's resources every day. The mindless consumptivism of wanting and acquiring more and more things and of using more and more resources must be rejected by every Christian, no matter how hard peers and advertisers push us in these directions. In its place, we must practice meeting essential needs of food, clothing, shelter and transportation carefully and efficiently and reusing and recycling what we do use as much and as often as possible. We ought to do all we can to make the places we live beautiful by including the beauty of other living things in and around our homes. And we ought to make our homes themselves match the characteristics of God's creation around them. As we practice these things individually, we also ought to practice them together, in churches and all Christian organizations, so that groups and places people identify with Christians show the truth of what we say about God's creation.

Third, we must speak faithfully about God's creation and our responsibility for it. What shall we say? That is the question this book has attempted to begin to answer, but four essential statements capture our witness in words: (1) God is Creator, and the universe, including humanity, is his creation; (2) we are linked to creation in many ways, both physically and spiritually, and therefore we must think and act in ways which take these linkages seriously; (3) we are distinct from other creatures by being made in the image of God, and we are called to express the distinction of that image by ruling and subduing creation. Following Christ's instruction (Matthew 20:25-28) and example (John 13:1-15), we understand that we express our authority by serving our subjects (creation), considering its needs first, acting deliberately to meet such needs in cultivating and preserving the earth (Genesis 2:15). And (4) we proclaim God as Redeemer (from sin) and creation, including humanity, as objects of his redemption accomplished in Christ (Romans 8:19-22). Human acts for creation's good are not the same as redemption, which is an act of God. But such acts receive lasting purpose and value when they are performed in obedience to God and within his redemptive purpose.

We ought to say these things as individuals (in ordinary conversation), as churches (in the pulpit and in Sunday school) and in other Christian organizations (in organizational statement, policy and practice). When we begin to do this, we will have begun to faithfully express our witness to others about who God is and what he has made.

Our Response: A Final Analysis
In *Pollution and the Death of Man,* the late Francis Schaeffer discussed the implications of an important article published in *Saturday Review,* entitled "Why Worry About Nature?" The author, sociologist Richard Means, suggested that the ecological crisis was really a moral crisis, and that a solution to it would be found in pantheism. Means said, "What, then, is the moral crisis? It is, I think, a pragmatic problem."[28]

Schaeffer responded, "Here was a remarkable combination of phrases; the moral dissolved into the pragmatic. He started off with a moral crisis, but suddenly all one is left with is a pragmatic problem."[29] Schaeffer continued,

The only reason we are called upon to treat nature well is because of its effects on man, and my children, and the generations to come. So in reality, in spite of all Means' words, man is left with a completely egoistic position in regard to nature. No reason is given—moral or logical—for regarding nature as something in itself. We are left with a purely pragmatic issue.[30]

The outcome of such thinking is well summarized by Schaeffer himself: "The . . . thing to notice is that what one has here is sociological religion and sociological science. . . . One does not have religion as religion; nor does one have science as science. What one has is both religion and science being used and manipulated for sociological purposes."[31]

We began this chapter by considering the content of a letter published by Carl Sagan, appealing for a joint commitment by science and religion to preserve and cherish the earth.[32] Now, having reviewed the key points of what a Christian environmental ethic is all about, it is time to return to it. Sagan's appeal has many things to commend it. It recognizes the present and historical reality of religion and the effect of faith on human life. This is a dramatic change from many scientific writers, who if they acknowledge religion as an influence at all, usually express the hope that someday it will go away. Sagan's letter is also commendable because it implicitly admits, by appealing to religion, that science and technology alone are insufficient to solve the environmental dilemma. This is a clear-sighted perception and a remarkable admission from a recognized spokesman for science. Finally, Sagan's appeal is commendable because it is expressed in a way that is gracious, courteous and sincere, rather than being condescending, rude and shallow. The appeal itself acknowledges the possibility for dialogue and interaction between science and religion, and for greater understanding between them.

Appreciating the positive aspects of Carl Sagan's appeal, we must recognize, at the same time, some of its shortcomings. This is not because we want to be picky or polemic, but because it is in this recognition that we come to understand most clearly what a truly Christian environmental ethic is and what it is not.

Sagan acknowledges that "religious teaching, example, and leadership are powerfully able to influence personal conduct and commitment."[33] This is true—in fact, unarguable. But religion in general, and Christianity in particular, is more than teaching, example and leadership, and faith is more than just one more behavior-modification device. Living faith produces virtuous behavior, including virtuous behavior toward God's creation. But it is not the behavior that makes the faith valuable. Faith is to be valued not because of its behavioral influences but because it provides real insights into the nature of God and of reality that a lack of faith cannot. In other words, faith has value because it is true, and because it genuinely has the power to change merely nice people (or perhaps nasty people) into new creations, and because it is the right response to the God of the universe in whom "we live and move and have our being" (Acts 17:28).

Of course we can produce such desirable behavior, or at least controllable behavior, through drugs or propaganda. This is exactly what is done to George Orwell's hero, Winston, in *1984*. But an Orwellian dictatorship is not what most people have in mind when they imagine an ideal society, because there is nothing ideal about getting people to do the right things for the wrong reasons.

As Christians, we must make clear, and require the scientific establishment to acknowledge, that faith lays claim to real truth, truth that affects not merely human behavior but the practice of science itself. We must ourselves understand and be able to graciously make clear to others, including Carl Sagan, what Paul means when he writes, "For by him [Christ] all things were created: things in heaven and on earth, visible and invisible, whether thrones or powers or rulers or authorities; all things were created by him and for him" (Colossians 1:16). The cosmos is not all that is, all that ever was or all that ever will be. Christ stands not only as its Creator but also as its Consummator—not only the One who began its existence but also the goal toward which it moves. We cannot insist that all scientists believe this, but we must make clear that faith is about something real, not merely a means to produce the right behavioral results in a good cause.

If we fail to do this, we will be but one short step away from the kind of "ecological religion" proposed by environmental philosophers like Garrett Hardin. Hardin has urged that we *reshape* (Hardin's word) humanity into "mature" creatures who no longer depend on the support of God (whom Hardin refers to as "Providence"). This will be done by embracing ecology *as* religion and then adhering to its two major dogmas: (1) not all things are possible and (2) the world is limited—therefore, demand must be restrained.[34]

Our ecologic crisis represents more than "crimes against creation." Indeed, it is meaningless to speak of a creation without reference to a

Creator, and the crimes to which Sagan refers are primarily crimes against God. The only way that religion has been able to influence "personal conduct and commitment" is to convince individuals of the reality of a Creator God who is also their Judge, to whom they will one day give account. Without a God who is also Creator there can be no creation, and without a God who is holy there can be no crime.

Finally, we must understand what is sacred and what is not. Sagan will be disappointed in the Christian witness if he hopes that we will teach others that the earth is sacred. This we cannot do, for sacredness can be ascribed ultimately only to God. The ground on which Moses stood was holy because God was present in the burning bush on it, not because of any inherent sacredness of soil. The creation, including this earth, is not to be well treated because it is sacred or because it should be worshiped, but because God made it and called it good (Genesis 1), and its goodness is independent of human utility.[35] Likewise, we value creation because God finds pleasure in it, and to so value creation is an act of honoring God. We also value and love God's creation because he intends to redeem it. And we, being creatures ourselves, will be redeemed with it.

It is sometimes possible to influence personal conduct and commitment by erecting an idol, but it is never wise. Christians cannot offer to other men and women the graven image of a "sacred" earth so that they will bow down before it and treat it well. This would be devious and false. Christians can offer only One who is himself sacred. Through obedience to him we can learn to love a creation that is precious to him and of which we are a part.

These distinctions are not made contentiously. In any case, no one can expect a single letter to address all the implications of an appeal for such a joint commitment as Carl Sagan has proposed. But sooner or later, these distinctions must be addressed, for such distinctions lie at the heart of Christian witness, as well as at the heart of what a genuinely Christian environmental ethic really is. They are necessary for the integrity of what Christianity is, and if the truth be known, they are necessary to the integrity of what science is. We must escape the trap of "sociological science" which Francis Schaeffer correctly perceived in the pantheistic solution of Richard Means: no science as science, no religion as religion, only science and religion used to manipulate humanity for a predetermined sociological purpose.

Such manipulation may not be Carl Sagan's intent. We assume that it is not. We only warn him, as we should warn others, to beware. Such snares as these show no partiality for their victims, whether they are ordinary Christians or great scientists. To both, Christian faith offers a different appeal. It is an appeal to take seriously the claims of God: about himself, about us and about his creation. If there would be true "environmental law," it cannot consist merely of rules supported by force. The authority of true environmental law (or better, *creation* law) must be moral, not merely coercive. It must persuade minds, not merely punish criminals. And the ultimate authority on which it stands must reflect genuine righteousness, not simply brute strength. It is on this authority, the Word of God and the resurrection of his Son Jesus Christ, that we place our trust. In this lies our one true hope.

A Mustard Seed Begins to Grow

Max Oelschlaeger is not a household name, but he is one of the most well-known, well-respected and well-published scholars in the field of environmental ethics. For many years Oelschlaeger took the view, with Lynn White Jr. and others, that the Judeo-Christian ethic was the cause of humanity's abuse of creation, that biblical teachings were the root of the environmental crisis.

In 1994 Yale University Press published Oelschlaeger's work *Caring for Creation*. This book opens with a stunning confession:

> For most of my adult life, I believed, as many environmentalists do, that religion was the primary cause of the ecologic crisis. I also assumed that various experts had solutions to the environmental malaise. I was a true believer. . . .
>
> I lost that faith by bits and pieces . . . by discovering the roots of my prejudice against religion. That bias grew out of my reading of Lynn White's famous essay blaming Judeo-Christianity for the environmental crisis.[36]

After a review of the major global environmental crises and the failure of both past and present environmental ethics (and ethicists) to solve them, Oelschlaeger makes a startling statement: "The church may be, in fact, our last, best chance. My conjecture is this: *There are no solutions for the systemic causes of ecocrisis, at least in democratic societies, apart from religious narrative*" (emphasis his).[37]

On paper, these are only words. But in one man's life, a world of thought suddenly has been altered. In the world of ideas, the foundations have been shaken.

But these are not the only eyes that now see things differently. Another long-time critic of the Judeo-Christian ethic, philosopher and environmental ethicist J. Baird Callicott, recently penned these words in his own book regarding religion and the ecologic crisis: "It is time the Judeo-Christian ethic of stewardship got the intellectual respect it deserves."[38] And the 1994 text of *Conservation Biology*, edited by Gary K. Meffe and C. Ronald Carroll, contains a chapter, also by Callicott, on conservation values and ethics. In that chapter Callicott devotes an entire section entitled "The Judeo-Christian Stewardship Conservation Ethic" to examining the biblical roots of the stewardship concept and its applications to modern conservation biology. Here Callicott writes, "The Judeo-Christian Stewardship Environmental Ethic is especially elegant and powerful. It also exquisitely matches the ethical requirements of conservation biology. The Judeo-Christian Stewardship Environmental Ethic confers objective value on nature in the clearest and most unambiguous of ways: by divine decree."[39]

These are not new ideas. They were only temporarily forgotten ones which, except for a recent brief interval, have shaped the wisdom and traditions of many centuries of scholarship. For more than thirty years secularism has had its way in culture and education in the Western world, and it has made a hash of both. Because secularism is, at root, both antihistory and antitradition, it forgot or ignored the rich heritage of Judeo-Christian teaching about humanity's stewardship of creation. It ignored not only biblical revelation but also the rich traditions of Western scholarship in science and ethics, which was informed and molded by that revelation.

In *Nature's Economy: A History of Ecological Ideas*, Donald Worster summarizes the views on this subject of the father of scientific nomenclature, Carolus Linnaeus. He quotes from Linnaeus's essay "The Oeconomy of Nature": "We understand the all-wise disposition of the Creator in relation to natural things, by which they are fitted to produce general ends, and reciprocal uses." Linnaeus believed that in God's design all creatures "are so connected, so chained together, that they all aim at the same end, and to this end a vast number of intermediate ends are subservient." So it was that the search for these general ends, for overriding purpose and agency in nature, became one of the prime motivators of an "ecological" (originally "economical") approach to the study of natural history.[40]

We, the authors of this book, have always believed in such a reawakening, such a rediscovery of the roots of both the foundations of ethics and the integrity of scientific inquiry. What is false cannot triumph forever. Someday the dawn must break.

Ironically, even Christians sometimes criticize other Christians who declare the Bible's witness to the human responsibility for creation's care, and do so for "economic" reasons.[41] But the "economy" of the modern world is an artifact of human construction, an anthropocentric value system that makes a modern and intellectually impoverished view of "economics" the measure of all things. It is a million miles from the "oeconomy" that Linnaeus spoke of, an oeconomy that came from God, was designed by God and revealed the attributes and intentions of God to those who gave attention to it. Modern economic systems, even if espoused from the pulpit, follow a thoroughly secularist pattern in ignoring the historical tradition of biblically informed Christian scholarship. In contrast, older views formed a tradition of scholarship that saw the connectedness (or, better, "economy") of all things. It is present not only in the writings of Linnaeus but also in outstanding works like John Ray's *The Wisdom of God Manifested in the Works of Creation* (1691), William Derham's *Physico-theology* (1713), William Paley's *Natural Theology* (1802) and the Bridgewater Treatises (1833-1836). To quote John Wesley, who wrote on the subject of ecology, "The design and will of the Creator is the only physical cause of the general economy of the world."[42]

But regardless of what human opinion is at any one moment, God's Word cannot be hindered. The light that it represents will never be swallowed up in darkness, no matter how well-funded or well-published that darkness may be. A new day is coming, and it reveals a new landscape. Christian thought and Christian practice will emerge again as the standard of moral excellence, not merely in theological journals but also in public debate. The biblical principles of Christian environmental stewardship will again shape not only thought and principles but the very policies of land and resource management. And the day is coming when Christian scholars and scientists will build the graduate training programs at Christian colleges and universities that will produce a new generation of resource managers and policymakers: women and men who are not compulsive careerists but sacrificial stewards—biblically informed, morally responsible and passionately devoted. It is their voices and their lives that will shape the future of ethics, policy and management of God's creation. Welcome to the new world.

Questions for Thought and Discussion

1. From your own study of this book and the biblical sources it cites, what makes a Christian environmental ethic *credible*? What actions could you take to make that environmental ethic more *plausible* to your own neighbors?

2. How would you distinguish a careerist from a steward? What do you think the church's role in training stewards should be?

3. What are the most important ideas the church can bring to the environmental debate? What would be the best channels for the church to express those ideas?

4. What idea, example or insight gained in or from this book has been most important to you? Why?

Appendix

Christian Denominational &
Interdenominational Groups Involved
with Environmental & Ecological Issues

American Baptist Churches, USA
Environmental Justice Dept.
P.O. Box 851
Valley Forge, PA 19482
(215) 768-2459

Appalachia—Science in the
  Public Interest (ASPI)
P.O. Box 298
Livingston, KY 40445

Au Sable Institute
Rt. 1, Big Twin Lake
Mancelona, MI 49652
(606) 587-8686

Catholic Fund for Overseas
  Development (CAFOD)
2 Romero Close
Stockwell Rd.
London SW9 9TY
UNITED KINGDOM

Catholic Relief Services
c/o Dr. Tom Remington
209 W. Fayette St.
Baltimore, MD 21201
(410) 625-2220 x3451

Center for Concern
3700 13th St. NE
Washington, DC 20016
(202) 635-2757

Center for the Respect of Life
  and Environment
2100 L St. NW
Washington, DC 20037
(202) 452-1100

Christian Ecology Group
115 Hawthorn Rd.
Kettering
Northants, England NN15 7HU
UNITED KINGDOM

Christian Environmental
  Association
1650 Zanker Rd.
San Jose, CA 9512-1129
(408) 441-0247

Christian Society of the Green
  Cross
10 E. Lancaster Ave.
Wynnewood, PA 19096
(610) 645-9393

Church Land Project
National Catholic Rural Life
  Conference
c/o Julia Kleinschmit
4625 Beaver Ave.
Des Moines, IA 50310
(515) 270-2634

Church of the Brethren
World Ministries Commission
Eco-Justice and Rural Crisis
  Dept.
1451 Dundee Ave.
Elgin, IL 60120
(847) 742-5100

Coordination in Development
  (CODEL)
Environment and Develop
  ment Committee
475 Riverside Dr.
New York, NY 10115
(212) 870-3000

Creation Song Radio
Rt. 1, Box 119-B
Dunmore, WV 24934
(304) 799-4137

ECHO (Educational Concerns
  Hunger Organization)
R.R. 2, Box 852
North Fort Myers, FL 33903
(813) 997-4713

Eco-Justice Project and Network
Attn: Dana Horrell
Anabel Taylor Hall
Cornell University
Ithaca, NY 14853-1001
(607) 255-4225

Episcopal Church
  Environmental Issues Desk
815 Second Ave.
New York, NY 10017
(212) 922-5223

Evangelical Environmental
  Network
10 Lancaster Ave.
Wynnewood, PA 19096
(610) 645-9392

Floresta
Bob Ainsworth, Directo
2820 Camino del Rio So.,
  Suite 300
San Diego, CA 92108-3824
(619) 298-7727

Friends Committee on Unity
with Nature
Isabel Bliss, Clerk
770 Clarks Lake Rd.
Chelsea, MI 48118

International Coordinating
Committee on Religion
and the Environment
(ICCRE)
Wainwright House
260 Stuyvesant Ave.
Rye, NY 10580
(914) 967-6080

International Network for
Religion and Animals
2913 Woodstock Ave.
Silver Spring, MD 20910
(301) 565-9132

Evangelical Lutheran Church
in America (ELCA)
Environmental Stewardship
Dept.
8765 W. Higgins Rd.
Chicago, IL 60641
(800) NET-ELCA Ext. 2708

Grassroots Coalition for
Environmental and
Economic Justice
P.O. Box 1319
Clarksville, MD 21029
(301) 964-3574

Greek Orthodox Archdiocese
of North America
Ecumenical Office
8-10 E. 79th St.
New York, NY 10021
(212) 570-3500

Interfaith Coalition on Energy
(ICE)
P.O. Box 26577
Philadelphia, PA 19141
(212) 635-1122

Living Water Contemplative
Center
P.O. Box 997
West Yellowstone, MT 59758

National Catholic Rural Life
Conference
Br. David Andrews, Executive
Director
4625 Beaver Ave.
Des Moines, IA 50310
(515) 270-2634

National Conference of
Catholic Women
c/o Sheila McCarron, Program
Director
1275 K St. NW
Washington, DC 20005
(202) 682-0334

National Religious Partnership
for the Environment
Paul Gorman, Executive
Director
1047 Amsterdam Ave.
New York, NY 10025
(212) 316-7325

Noah's Ark
c/o Les Braund
8858 Capcano Rd.
San Diego, CA 92126
(619) 566-3958

North American Coalition
on Religion and Ecology
5 Thomas Circle
Washington, DC 20005

Presbyterian Church USA
Office of Environmental
Justice
100 Witherspoon St., Rm. 3046
Louisville, KY 40202
(502) 569-5809

Quaker Peace and Service
Friends House
Euston Rd.
London NW1 2BJ
UNITED KINGDOM

René Dubos Consortium
for Sacred Ecology
c/o St. John the Divine Cathedral
1047 Amsterdam Ave.
New York, NY 10025
(212) 316-7400

Servants in Faith and Technology
(SIFAT)
Rev. Kenneth Carson
Rt. 1, Box D-14
Lineville, AL 36266
(205) 396-2017

Sierra Treks
Dave Willis
15187 Greensprings Hwy.
Ashland, OR 97520
(503) 482-2307 or 482-0526

Southern Baptist Convention
Christian Life Commission
901 Commerce St., Suite 550
Nashville, TN 37203-3696
(615) 244-2495

United Methodist Church
General Board of Church
and Society
c/o Jaydee Hanson
100 Maryland Ave. NE
Washington, DC 20002

United Methodist Rural
  Fellowship
c/o Melvin West
108 Balow Wynd
Columbia, MO 64203
(314) 445-9397

United Church of Christ
Office of Church and Society
110 Maryland Ave. NE
Washington, DC 20002
(202) 543-1517

U.S. Catholic Conference
Eco-Justice Department
Fr. Drew Christiansen, S.J.
3211 4th St. NE
Washington, DC 20016
(202) 541-3140

Wilderness Manna
Environmental Ministry
1404 Arnold Ave.
San Jose, CA 95110
(408) 451-9310

Notes

Chapter 1: A Creation in Crisis

[1]Peter Kalm, *Travels into North America,* quoted in Joseph M. Petulla, *American Environmental History* (San Francisco: Boyd and Fraser, 1977), p. 56.

[2]Frank Graham Jr., *The Adirondack Park: A Political History* (New York: Alfred A. Knopf, 1978), pp. 66-67.

[3]Elaine M. Murphy, *World Population: Toward the Next Century* (Washington, D.C.: Population Reference Bureau, 1985), p. 1.

[4]Susan P. Bratton, *Six Billion and More: Human Population Regulation and Christian Ethics* (Louisville, Ky.: Westminster/John Knox, 1992), p. 15.

[5]G. Tyler Miller Jr., *Living in the Environment,* 7th ed. (Belmont, Calif.: Wadsworth, 1992), p. 5.

[6]Robert Farmighetti, ed., *The World Almanac and Book of Facts 1995* (Mahwah, N.J.: Funk and Wagnall's, 1994), pp. 839-41.

[7]Ibid., p. 840.

[8]Ibid., p. 841.

[9]William K. Stevens, "Threat of Encroaching Deserts May Be More Myth Than Fact," *The New York Times,* January 18, 1994.

[10]"Desertification Convention Adopted," *UN Chronicle* 31, no. 3 (1994): 74.

[11]Lewis J. Perelman, *The Global Mind: Beyond the Limits to Growth* (New York: Mason/Charter, 1976).

[12]Richard A. Houghton and George M. Woodwell, "Global Climatic Change," *Scientific American* 260, no. 4 (1989): 36-44.

[13]John R. Sheaffer and Raymond H. Brand, *Whatever Happened to Eden?* (Wheaton, Ill.: Tyndale House, 1980), p. 98.

[14]Garrett Hardin, "The Tragedy of the Commons," *Science* 162 (1968): 1243-49.

Chapter 2: God the Creator

[1]Francis Schaeffer, *Pollution and the Death of Man: The Christian View of Ecology* (Wheaton, Ill.: Tyndale House, 1973), p. 47.

[2]Joan O'Brien and Wildred Major, *In the Beginning: Creation Myths from Ancient Mesopotamia, Israel and Greece* (Chico, Calif.: Scholars Press, 1982), p. 25.

[3]Ibid., pp. 70-84.

[4]Ibid., p. 115.

[5]Ibid.

[6]M. B. Foster, "The Christian Doctrine of Creation and the Rise of Modern Science," in *Creation: The Impact of an Idea*, ed. D. O'Connor and F. Oakley (New York: Charles Scribner's Sons, 1968), pp. 29-53.

[7]Schaeffer, *Pollution and the Death of Man*, p. 47.

[8]Dietrich Bonhoeffer, *Creation and Fall: A Theological Interpretation of Genesis 1—3* (London: SCM Press, 1960), pp. 20-21.

[9]Daniel O'Connor, "Introduction: The Human and the Divine," in *Creation: The Impact of an Idea*, ed. D. O'Connor and F. Oakley (New York: Charles Scribner's Sons, 1968), pp. 107-19.

[10]Fred G. Van Dyke, Arlan J. Birkey and Ted D. Nickel, "Integration and the Christian College: Reflection on the Nineteenth Psalm," in *The Best in Theology*, ed. J. I. Packer (Carol Stream, Ill.: Christianity Today, 1989), 3:399.

[11]Some commentators think it is a hippopotamus, but in any event it is a great and powerful beast.

[12]James A. Nash, *Loving Nature: Ecological Integrity and Christian Responsibility* (Nashville: Abingdon, 1991), p. 95.

Chapter 3: The Value of Creation
[1]Fred G. Van Dyke, Arlan J. Birkey and Ted D. Nickel, "Integration and the Christian College: Reflection on the Nineteenth Psalm," in *The Best in Theology*, ed. J. I. Packer (Carol Stream, Ill.: Christianity Today, 1989), 3:395-400.

[2]Dietrich Bonhoeffer, *Creation and Fall: A Theological Interpretation of Genesis 1—3* (London: SCM Press, 1959), p. 15.

[3]Van Dyke, Birkey and Nickel, "Integration and the Christian College."

[4]Bonhoeffer, *Creation and Fall*, p. 32.

[5]John Naisbitt and Patricia Aburdene, *Megatrends: Ten New Directions Transforming Our Lives* (New York: Warner, 1982), pp. 222, 229.

[6]James R. Udall, "The Tucson Paradox," *Audubon* 87, no. 1 (1985): 98-99.

[7]Ibid., p. 98.

[8]Ibid., p. 99.

[9]Naisbitt, *Megatrends*, p. 229.

[10]Udall, "Tucson Paradox," p. 99.

[11]Ibid., p. 98.

[12]Wendell Berry, "Two Economies," *Review and Expositor* 81 (1984): 209-23.

[13]Nicholas Wolterstorff, *Until Justice and Peace Embrace* (Grand Rapids, Mich.: Eerdmans, 1983), p. 60.

[14]Tim Hermach, "The Great Tree Robbery," *The New York Times*, September 17, 1991.

[15]Ibid.

[16]Daniel L. Dustin and Leo H. McAvoy, "The Decline and Fall of Quality Recreation Opportunities and Environments," *Environmental Ethics,* Spring 1982, pp. 48-55.

[17]Ibid., p. 52.

[18]Ibid., p. 49.

[19]Ibid., p. 55.

[20]Aldo Leopold, *A Sand County Almanac: With Essays on Conservation from Round River* (New York: Sierra Club/Ballantine Books, 1974), p. 116.

[21]René Dubos, *Man Adapting* (New Haven, Conn.: Yale University Press, 1965), p. 279.

[22]Wendell Berry, *The Unsettling of America* (San Francisco: Sierra Club Books, 1977), pp. 27-28.

[23]Leopold, *Sand County Almanac,* p. 261.

[24]Dietrich Bonhoeffer, *Ethics* (New York: Macmillan, 1965), p. 15.

[25]Lynn White Jr., "The Historical Roots of Our Ecologic Crisis," *Science* 155 (1967): 1203-7.

[26]Julian L. Simon and Herman Kahn, introduction to *The Resourceful Earth: A Response to Global 2000,* ed. Julian L. Simon and Herman Kahn (Oxford: Blackwell, 1984), p. 23.

[27]Bonhoeffer, *Creation and Fall,* p. 28.

[28]Alston Chase, "How to Save Our National Parks," *The Atlantic* 260, no. 1 (1987): 35-44.

[29]C. S. Lewis, *The Great Divorce* (New York: Macmillan, 1954), p. 26.

Chapter 4: Out of the Dust

[1]Paulos Gregorios, *The Human Presence: An Orthodox View of Nature* (Geneva: World Council of Churches, 1978).

[2]Derek Kidner, *Genesis: An Introduction and Commentary* (Downers Grove, Ill.: InterVarsity Press, 1967), p. 43.

[3]Ibid., p. 50.

[4]Dietrich Bonhoeffer, *Creation and Fall: A Theological Interpretation of Genesis 1—3* (London: SCM Press, 1959), p. 20.

[5]Loren Wilkinson, "Global Housekeeping: Lords or Servants?" *Christianity Today* 24 (1980): 27.

[6]Paul Brand, "A Handful of Mud," *Christianity Today* 29 (1985): 28.

[7]Joseph Sittler, *Essays on Nature and Grace* (Philadelphia: Fortress, 1972).

[8]J. D. Douglas, ed., *The New Bible Dictionary* (Grand Rapids, Mich.: Eerdmans, 1962), p. 956.

[9]Nicholas Wolterstorff, *Until Justice and Peace Embrace* (Grand Rapids, Mich.: Eerdmans, 1983), p. 70.

[10]Walter Brueggemann, *Living Toward a Vision: Biblical Essays on Shalom* (New York: United Church Press, 1976), p. 15.

[11]Aldo Leopold, *A Sand County Almanac: With Essays on Conservation from Round*

River (New York: Sierra Club/Ballantine Books, 1974), pp. 256-57.

[12]Lynn White Jr., "The Historical Roots of Our Ecologic Crisis," *Science* 155 (1967): 1207.

[13]Henri Blocher, *In the Beginning* (Downers Grove, Ill.: InterVarsity Press, 1984), p. 184.

[14]John Currid, "The Deforestation of the Foothills of Palestine," *Palestine Exploration Quarterly* 16 (1984): 1.

[15]Dennis Baly, *The Geography of the Bible* (New York: Harper & Brothers, 1957), p. 92.

[16]George Adam Smith, *The Historical Geography of the Holy Land* (London: Hodder & Stoughton, 1902), p. 93.

[17]Ralph Smith, "Old Testament Concepts of Stewardship," *Southwestern Journal of Theology* 13 (Spring 1971): 7-13.

[18]Bonhoeffer, *Creation and Fall*, p. 23.

[19]Trophime Mouiren, *The Creation*, trans. S. J. Tester (New York: Hawthorn Books, 1962), p. 21.

[20]David Ehrenfeld, "Nature in the Jewish Tradition: The Source of Stewardship," in *Proceedings of the Au Sable Forum 1981: Redeeming the Earth* (Mancelona, Mich.: Au Sable Institute of Environmental Studies, 1981).

Chapter 5: Covenant & Redemption

[1]Dietrich Bonhoeffer, *Creation and Fall: A Theological Interpretation of Genesis 1—3* (London: SCM Press, 1959), p. 88.

[2]J. D. Douglas, ed., *The New Bible Dictionary* (Grand Rapids, Mich.: Eerdmans, 1962), p. 1189.

[3]G. R. Beasley-Murray, "The Revelation," in *The Eerdmans Bible Commentary*, ed. D. Guthrie and J. A. Motyer, 3rd ed. (Grand Rapids, Mich.: Eerdmans, 1970), p. 1287.

[4]Norman D. Levine, "Evolution and Extinction," *BioScience* 39 (1989): 38.

[5]Ibid.

[6]Norman Myers, "Extinction Rates Past and Present," *BioScience* 39 (1989): 39-41.

[7]Ibid.

[8]David Ehrenfeld, "The Business of Conservation," *Conservation Biology* 6 (1992): 1-3.

[9]Ibid., p. 2.

[10]Ibid.

[11]"Assassination of Brazilian Priest by Opponents of Land Reform," *LADOC: Bimonthly Publication of Latin American Documentation*, November-December 1986, p. 18.

[12]Thomas Berry, *The Dream of the Earth* (San Francisco: Sierra Club Books, 1988).

[13]Kenneth Woodward, "A New Story of Creation," *Newsweek* 113 (June 5, 1989): 72.

[14]Aldo Leopold, *A Sand County Almanac: With Essays on Conservation from Round River* (New York: Sierra Club/Ballantine Books, 1974), p. 246.

[15]Ibid.

[16]Karl Barth, *Church Dogmatics* 3/1: *The Work of Creation* (New York: T & T Clark, 1958), p. 181.

[17]Gerhard von Rad, *Genesis: A Commentary* (Philadelphia: Westminster Press, 1961), pp. 57-58.

[18]Bonhoeffer, *Creation and Fall*, pp. 95-96.

Chapter 6: Ruling & Subduing

[1]Lynn White Jr., "The Historical Roots of Our Ecologic Crisis," *Science* 155 (1967): 1206.

[2]Aldo Leopold, *A Sand County Almanac: With Essays on Conservation from Round River* (New York: Sierra Club/Ballantine Books, 1974), p. 240.

[3]Jack Cottrell, *What the Bible Says About God the Ruler* (Joplin, Mo.: College Press, 1984), p. 99.

[4]Leopold, *Sand County Almanac*.

[5]Francis A. Schaeffer, *Pollution and the Death of Man: The Christian View of Ecology* (Wheaton, Ill.: Tyndale House, 1969).

Chapter 7: God's World Today

[1]Jacques Ellul, *Money and Power* (Downers Grove, Ill.: InterVarsity Press, 1984), p. 19.

[2]Rachel Carson, *Silent Spring* (Boston: Houghton Mifflin, 1962).

[3]"World Food News Special Report: How Many People Can the World Feed?" *Population Today* 13, no. 1 (1985): 9.

[4]Ibid.

[5]Ibid.

[6]Lester Brown, ed., *State of the World 1985* (New York: W. W. Norton, 1985), p. 25.

[7]"The Food Crisis in Sub-Saharan Africa," *Population Education Newsletter* 14, no. 1 (1985).

[8]Garrett Hardin, "The Tragedy of the Commons," *Science* 162 (1968): 1243-48.

[9]William Cronon, *Changes in the Land: Indians, Colonists and the Ecology of New England* (New York: Hill and Wang, 1983).

[10]D. E. Gushess, "The Energy Options Before Us: A View from Capitol Hill," *ESA Advocate* 13, no. 6 (1991): 12-14.

[11]Peter Steinhart, "The Edge Gets Thinner," *Audubon* 85, no. 6 (1983): 105.

[12]Ibid., p. 102.

[13]Wendell Berry, "Two Economies," *Review and Expositor* 81 (1984): 212.

[14]Brown, *State of the World 1985*, p. 52.

[15]David Skole and Compton Tucker, "Tropical Deforestation and Habitat Fragmentation in the Amazon: Data from 1978 to 1988," *Science* 260 (1993): 1905-10.

[16]Brown, *State of the World 1985*, p. 11.

[17]"Two Say Politics Rule Their Agencies," *High Country News* 23, no. 18 (1991): 1, 10.

[18]J. M. Scott, B. Csuti and K. A. Smith, "Commentary: Playing Noah While Paying the Devil," *Bulletin of the Ecological Society of America* 71 (1990): 156-59.

[19]Richard B. Primack, *Essentials of Conservation Biology* (Sunderland, Mass.: Sinauer Associates, 1993).

[20]L. Tangley, "Cataloging Costa Rica's Diversity," *BioScience* 40, no. 9 (1990): 633-36.

[21]Anthony T. Jacob, *Acid Rain* (Madison, Wis.: Institute for Chemical Education, 1991), p. 2.

[22]Ibid.

[23]Ibid., p. 3.

[24]Richard A. Houghton, "The Role of Forests in Affecting the Greenhouse Gas Composition of the Atmosphere," in *Global Climate Change and Life on Earth*, ed. Richard L. Wyman (New York: Routledge, Chapman and Hall, 1991), pp. 43-55; Richard A. Houghton and George M. Woodwell, "Global Climatic Change," *Scientific American* 260, no. 4 (1989): 36-44; Stephen H. Schneider, "The Greenhouse Effect: Science and Policy," *Science* 243 (1989): 771-81; Peter M. Vitousek, "Beyond Global Warming: Ecology and Global Change," *Ecology* 75, no. 7 (1994): 1861-76.

[25]Richard T. Wetherald, introduction to *Global Climate Change and Life on Earth*, ed. Richard L. Wyman (New York: Routledge, Chapman and Hall, 1991), pp. 15-16.

[26]Ibid., pp. 4, 16.

[27]Ibid., p. 16.

[28]Kurt Kleiner, "Climate Change Threatens Southern Asia," *New Scientist* 143 (1994): 6.

[29]Ibid.

[30]Constance Holden, "Greening of the Antarctic Peninsula," *Science* 266 (1994): 35.

[31]Richard Monastersky, "Temperatures on the Rise in Deep Atlantic," *Science News* 145 (1994): 295.

[32]Johannes Oerlemans, "Quantifying Global Warming from the Retreat of Glaciers," *Science* 264 (1994): 243-45.

[33]John Timson, "Leafy Hordes Invade Arctic," *New Scientist* 141 (1994): 14.

[34]Jennifer L. Gross, "Flooding the Ocean," *Environment* 36, no. 3 (1994): 23-24; "Deforestation Leads to Sea Level Rise," *Geotimes* 39, no. 5 (1994): 9.

[35]Paul R. Ehrlich, "Foreword: Facing Up to Climate Change," in *Global Climate Change and Life on Earth*, ed. Richard L. Wyman (New York: Routledge, Chapman and Hall, 1991), pp. ix-xiii.

[36]G. Tyler Miller Jr., *Living in the Environment: Principles, Connections and Solutions*, 8th ed. (Belmont, Calif.: Wadsworth, 1994), p. 304.

[37]Pamela S. Zurer, "Ozone Depletion's Recurring Surprises Challenge Atmos-

pheric Scientists," *Chemical and Engineering News* 71, no. 21 (1993): 8-18.

[38]"The Word About Ozone," *Science News* 146 (1994): 187.

[39]Zurer, "Ozone Depletion's Recurring Surprises," p. 9.

[40]Ibid.

[41]Ibid.

Chapter 8: The Consequences of Disobedience

[1]Dietrich Bonhoeffer, *Creation and Fall: A Theological Interpretation of Genesis 1—3* (London: SCM Press, 1959), p. 82.

[2]Herman E. Daly, *Steady State Economics: The Economics of Biophysical Equilibrium and Moral Growth* (San Francisco: W. H. Freeman, 1977), p. 8.

[3]Zev Naveh, "Neot Kedumim," *Restoration and Management Notes* 7 (1989): 9-13.

[4]Ibid.

[5]G. Tyler Miller Jr., *Living in the Environment*, 7th ed. (Belmont, Calif.: Wadsworth, 1992), p. 589.

[6]Ibid.

[7]Ibid., p. 590.

[8]Wendell Berry, "Two Economies," *Review and Expositor* 81 (1984): 212.

[9]Miller, *Living in the Environment*, p. 586.

[10]Anthony T. Jacob, *Acid Rain* (Madison, Wis.: Institute for Chemical Education, 1991), p. 28.

[11]Miller, *Living in the Environment*, p. 570.

[12]Ibid.

[13]Mary Beck Desmond, "Global Environment: Earth Day 1990," *Earth Science* 43 (Spring 1990): 6.

[14]Joseph M. Petulla, *American Environmental History* (San Francisco: Boyd and Fraser, 1977), p. 189.

[15]S. R. Kellert and J. K. Berry, *Phase III: Knowledge, Affection and Basic Attitudes Toward Animals in American Society* (Arlington, Va.: National Technical Information Service, 1980).

[16]Lynn White Jr., "The Historical Roots of Our Ecologic Crisis," *Science* 155 (1967): 1203-7.

[17]Joseph K. Sheldon, *Rediscovery of Creation: A Bibliographical Study of the Church's Response to the Environmental Crisis* (Metuchen, N.J.: American Theological Library Association and Scarecrow Press, 1992).

[18]Constance Cumbey, *Hidden Dangers of the Rainbow: The New Age Movement and Our Coming Age of Barbarism* (Shreveport, La.: Huntington House, 1983).

[19]Richard T. Wright, *Biology Through the Eyes of Faith* (San Francisco: Harper & Row, 1989), pp. 177-78.

[20]Alexander Schmemann, *For the Life of the World: Sacraments and Orthodoxy* (Crestwood, N.Y.: St. Vladimir's Seminary Press, 1973), p. 118.

[21]Aldo Leopold, *A Sand County Almanac: With Essays on Conservation from Round River* (New York: Sierra Club/Ballantine Books, 1974), p. 239.

[22]Ibid., p. 238.

[23]Ibid., p. 240.

[24]Ibid., p. 246.

[25]Ibid.

[26]Ibid., p. 265.

[27]James H. Shaw, "Assessing the Progress Toward Leopold's Land Ethic," *Wildlife Society Bulletin* 15 (1987): 470-72.

[28]Ibid.

[29]Ibid.

[30]White, "Historical Roots," p. 1207.

[31]Randy Frame, "Protecting the Lord's Canvas," *Christianity Today* 32, no. 17 (1988): 74-75.

[32]Alston Chase, *Playing God in Yellowstone* (San Diego, Calif.: Harcourt Brace Jovanovich, 1987), p. 347.

[33]George Sessions and Bill Devall, *Deep Ecology: Living As If Nature Mattered* (Salt Lake City: Gibbs M. Smith, 1985).

[34]Chase, *Playing God in Yellowstone*, p. 335.

[35]Fred G. Van Dyke, "Beyond Sand County: A Biblical Perspective on Environmental Ethics," *Journal of the American Scientific Affiliation* 37 (1985): 40-48.

[36]Stephen Schneider and Penelope Boston, eds., *Scientists on Gaia* (Cambridge, Mass.: MIT Press, 1991), p. xiii.

[37]White, "Historical Roots," p. 1207.

[38]Wendell Berry, *The Unsettling of America* (San Francisco: Sierra Club Books, 1977), p. 7.

[39]James Gustafson, *Ethics from a Theocentric Perspective* (Chicago: University of Chicago Press, 1981), p. 109.

Chapter 9: A Christian Response

[1]Roy J. Enquist, "A Paraclete in the Public Square: Toward a Theology of Advocacy," *Theology and Public Policy* 2 (1990): 21-27.

[2]Joseph K. Sheldon, *Rediscovery of Creation: A Bibliographical Study of the Church's Response to the Environmental Crisis* (Metuchen, N.J.: American Theological Library Association and Scarecrow Press, 1992).

[3]Ian McHarg, *Design with Nature* (Garden City, N.Y.: Natural History Press, 1969).

[4]Raymond H. Brand, "At the Point of Need," *Perspectives on Science and Christian Faith* 39 (1987): 3-8.

[5]"Two Say Politics Rule Their Agencies," *High Country News* 33, no. 18 (1991): 1, 10-12.

[6]Ibid., p. 12.

[7]Ibid.

[8]Ibid., p. 11.

[9]Paul Schneider, "When a Whistle Blows in the Forest," *Audubon* 94, no. 1 (1992): 42-49.

[10]Michael Lipske, "Who Runs America's Forests?" *National Wildlife* 28, no. 6 (1990): 24-34.

[11]Randall O'Toole, "Recreation Fees and the Yellowstone Forests," in *The Greater Yellowstone Ecosystem: Redefining America's Wilderness Heritage*, ed. Robert B. Keiter and Mark S. Boyce (New Haven, Conn.: Yale University Press, 1991), pp. 41-48.

[12]Ibid., p. 43.

[13]Ibid.

[14]Schneider, "When a Whistle Blows."

[15]Alston Chase, *Playing God in Yellowstone* (San Diego, Calif.: Harcourt Brace Jovanovich, 1987).

[16]Ed Marston, "Will the Bush Administration Choose Reform?" *High Country News* 33, no. 18 (1991): 13.

[17]Alasdair MacIntyre, *After Virtue* (South Bend, Ind.: Notre Dame University Press, 1981), p. 236.

[18]Stephen V. Monsma, *Pursuing Justice in a Sinful World* (Grand Rapids, Mich.: Eerdmans, 1984).

[19]O'Toole, "Recreation Fees."

[20]Chase, *Playing God in Yellowstone.*

[21]Joseph L. Sax, "Ecosystem and Property Rights in Greater Yellowstone: The Legal System in Transition," in *The Greater Yellowstone Ecosystem: Redefining America's Wilderness Heritage*, ed. Robert B. Keiter and Mark S. Boyce (New Haven, Conn.: Yale University Press, 1991), pp. 77-84.

[22]Garrett Hardin, "The Tragedy of the Commons," *Science* 162 (1968): 1243-48.

[23]David Halvarg, *The War Against the Greens: The "Wise-Use" Movement, the New Right and Anti-environmental Violence* (San Francisco: Sierra Club Books, 1994).

[24]Aldo Leopold, *A Sand County Almanac: With Essays on Conservation from Round River* (New York: Sierra Club/Ballantine Books, 1974), p. 246.

[25]James R. Newby and Elizabeth S. Newby, *Between Peril and Promise* (Nashville: Thomas Nelson, 1984), pp. 84-85.

Chapter 10: Ecology & the Christian Mind

[1]Montaigne, *Essays,* trans. John Florio (New York: Everyman's Library, 1965), p. 144.

[2]Carl Sagan, "Guest Comment: Preserving and Cherishing the Earth—An Appeal for Joint Commitment in Science and Religion," *American Journal of Physics* 58 (1990): 615.

[3]Ibid.

[4]Ibid.

[5]Ibid.

[6]Mary Beck Desmond, "Global Environment: Earth Day 1990," *Earth Science* 43 (Spring 1990): 7.

[7]Ibid.

[8]René Dubos, *Beast or Angel? Choices That Make Us Human* (New York: Charles Scribner's Sons, 1974), p. 43.

[9]Ibid., p. 41.

[10]Lynn White Jr., "The Historical Roots of Our Ecologic Crisis," *Science* 155 (1967): 1204-7.

[11]Jonathan Edwards, *Charity and Its Fruits* (Edinburgh: Banner of Truth Trust, 1969), pp. 157-58.

[12]Garrett Hardin, "The Tragedy of the Commons," *Science* 162 (1968): 1243-48.

[13]Joseph M. Petulla, *American Environmental History* (San Francisco: Boyd and Fraser, 1977), p. 47.

[14]Ibid., p. 56.

[15]James M. Gustafson, *Ethics from a Theocentric Perspective* (Chicago: University of Chicago Press, 1981), pp. 23-24.

[16]J. I. Packer, *Knowing God* (Downers Grove, Ill.: InterVarsity Press, 1973), p. 254.

[17]Daniel O'Connor and Francis Oakley, eds., *Creation: The Impact of an Idea* (New York: Charles Scribner's Sons, 1969).

[18]Fred G. Van Dyke, "Beyond Sand County: A Christian Perspective On Environmental Ethics," *Journal of the American Scientific Affiliation* 37 (1985): 40-48.

[19]Au Sable Institute, *Official Bulletin 1993* (Mancelona, Mich.: Au Sable Institute of Environmental Studies, 1992), p. i.

[20]C. S. Lewis, *The Abolition of Man* (New York: Macmillan, 1947), p. 34.

[21]Ibid., pp. 30-31.

[22]Wendell Berry, *The Unsettling of America* (San Francisco: Sierra Club Books, 1972), p. 169.

[23]Peter Berger, *A Rumor of Angels* (Garden City, N.Y.: Archer Books, 1970).

[24]Ronald J. Sider, *Rich Christians in an Age of Hunger* (Downers Grove, Ill.: InterVarsity Press, 1977).

[25]Richard John Neuhaus, *The Naked Public Square* (Grand Rapids, Mich.: Eerdmans, 1984).

[26]Roy J. Enquist, "A Paraclete in the Public Square: Toward a Theology of Advocacy," *Theology and Public Policy* 2 (1990): 21-27.

[27]Os Guinness, *The Gravedigger File* (Downers Grove, Ill.: InterVarsity Press, 1983).

[28]Richard L. Means, "Why Worry About Nature?" *Saturday Review,* December 2, 1967.

[29]Francis A. Schaeffer, *Pollution and the Death of Man: The Christian View of Ecology* (Wheaton, Ill.: Tyndale House, 1970), p. 20.

[30]Ibid., pp. 26-27.

[31]Ibid., p. 29.

[32]Sagan, "Guest Comment: Preserving and Cherishing the Earth."

[33]Ibid.

[34]Garrett Hardin, "Ecology and the Death of Providence," *Zygon* 15 (1980):

57-68.

[35]Van Dyke, "Beyond Sand County."

[36]Max Oelschlaeger, *Caring for Creation: An Ecumenical Approach to the Environmental Crisis* (New Haven, Conn.: Yale University Press, 1994), p. 1.

[37]Ibid., p. 5.

[38]J. Baird Callicott, *World Views and Ecology* (Lewisburg, Penn.: Bucknell University Press, 1993), p. 18.

[39]J. Baird Callicott, "Conservation Values and Ethics," in *Principles of Conservation Biology,* ed. Gary K. Meffe and C. Ronald Carroll (Sunderland, Mass.: Sinauer Associates, 1994), p. 36.

[40]Donald Worster, *Nature's Economy: A History of Ecological Ideas* (New York: Cambridge University Press, 1977), pp. 37-38.

[41]E. Calvin Beisner, *Prospects for Growth: A Biblical View of Population, Resources and the Future* (Westchester, Ill.: Crossway, 1990); Larry Burkett, *Whatever Happened to the American Dream?* (Chicago: Moody Press, 1993).

[42]Worster, *Nature's Economy,* p. 38.

Bibliography

Au Sable Institute of Environmental Studies. *Official Bulletin 1993*, vol. 1. Mancelona, Mich.: Au Sable Institute, 1992.

Baly, Dennis. *The Geography of the Bible*. New York: Harper & Brothers, 1957.

Barth, Karl. *Church Dogmatics 3/1: The Work of Creation*. New York: T & T Clark, 1958.

Beasley-Murray, G. R. "The Revelation." In *The Eerdmans Bible Commentary*, pp. 1279-310. Edited by Donald Guthrie and J. A. Motyer. 3rd ed. Grand Rapids, Mich.: Eerdmans, 1970.

Berger, Peter. *A Rumor of Angels*. Garden City, N.Y.: Anchor Books, 1970.

Berry, Thomas. *The Dream of the Earth*. San Francisco: Sierra Club Books, 1988.

Berry, Wendell. "Two Economies." *Review and Expositor* 81 (1984): 209-23.

_____. *The Unsettling of America*. San Francisco: Sierra Club Books, 1977.

Blocher, Henri. *In the Beginning*. Downers Grove, Ill.: InterVarsity Press, 1984.

Bonhoeffer, Dietrich. *Creation and Fall: A Theological Interpretation of Genesis 1—3*. London: SCM Press, 1960.

_____. *Ethics*. New York: Macmillan, 1965.

Brand, Paul. "A Handful of Mud." *Christianity Today* 29 (1985): 25-31.

Brand, Raymond H. "At the Point of Need." *Perspectives on Science and Christian Faith* 39 (1987): 3-8.

Bratton, Susan P. *Six Billion and More: Human Population and Christian Ethics*. Louisville, Ky.: Westminster/John Knox Press, 1992.

Brown, Lester R., ed. *State of the World 1985*. New York: W. W. Norton, 1985.

Brueggemann, Walter. *Living Toward a Vision: Biblical Essays on Shalom*. New York: United Church Press, 1976.

Burton, John, ed. *The Atlas of Endangered Species*. New York: Macmillan, 1991.

Carson, Rachel. *Silent Spring*. Boston: Houghton Mifflin, 1962.

Chase, Alston. "How to Save Our National Parks." *The Atlantic* 260, no. 1 (1987): 35-44.

_____. *Playing God in Yellowstone*. San Diego, Calif.: Harcourt Brace Jovanovich, 1987.

Cottrell, Jack. *What the Bible Says About God the Ruler.* Joplin, Mo.: College Press, 1984.

Cronin, William. *Changes in the Land: Indians, Colonists and the Ecology of New England.* New York: Hill and Wang, 1983.

Cumbey, Constance. *Hidden Dangers of the Rainbow: The New Age Movement and Our Coming Age of Barbarism.* Shreveport, La.: Huntington House, 1983.

Currid, John. "The Deforestation of the Foothills of Palestine." *Palestine Exploration Quarterly* 16 (1984): 1-11.

Daly, Herman E. *Steady State Economics: The Economics of Biophysical Equilibrium and Moral Growth.* San Francisco: W. H. Freeman, 1977.

Desmond, Mary Beck. "Global Environment: Earth Day 1990." *Earth Science* 43 (Spring 1990): 6-7.

Douglas, J. D., ed. *The New Bible Dictionary.* Grand Rapids, Mich.: Eerdmans, 1962.

Dubos, René. *Beast or Angel? Choices That Make Us Human.* New York: Charles Scribner's Sons, 1974.

_____. *Man Adapting.* New Haven, Conn.: Yale University Press, 1965.

Dustin, Daniel L., and Leo H. McAvoy. "The Decline and Fall of Quality Recreational Opportunities and Environments." *Environmental Ethics* 4 (1982): 48-55.

Ecological Society of America. *The Sustainable Biosphere Initiative.* Bethesda, Md.: Ecological Society of America, 1990.

Edwards, Jonathan. *Charity and Its Fruits.* Edinburgh: Banner of Truth Trust, 1969.

Ehrenfeld, David. "The Business of Conservation." *Conservation Biology* 6 (1992): 1-3.

_____. "Nature in the Jewish Tradition: The Source of Stewardship." In *Proceedings of the Au Sable Forum 1981: Redeeming the Earth.* Mancelona, Mich.: Au Sable Institute of Environmental Studies, 1981.

Ehrlich, Paul R. "Foreword: Facing Up to Climate Change." In *Global Climate Change and Life on Earth,* pp. ix-xiii. Edited by Richard L. Wyman. New York: Routledge, Chapman and Hall, 1991.

Ellul, Jacques. *Money and Power.* Downers Grove, Ill.: InterVarsity Press, 1984.

Enquist, Roy J. "A Paraclete in the Public Square: Toward a Theology of Advocacy." *Theology and Public Policy* 2 (1990): 21-27.

Foster, M. B. "The Christian Doctrine of Creation and the Rise of Modern Science." In *Creation: The Impact of an Idea,* pp. 29-53. Edited by Daniel O'Connor and Francis Oakley. New York: Charles Scribner's Sons, 1968.

Frame, Randy. "Protecting the Lord's Canvas." *Christianity Today* 32, no. 17 (1988): 74-75.

Graham, Frank, Jr. *The Adirondack Park: A Political History.* New York: Alfred A. Knopf, 1978.

Gregorios, Paulos. *The Human Presence: An Orthodox View of Nature.* Geneva: World Council of Churches, 1978.

Guinness, Os. *The Gravedigger File.* Downers Grove, Ill.: InterVarsity Press, 1983.

Gushess, D. E. "The Energy Options Before Us: A View from Capitol Hill." *ESA Advocate* 13, no. 6 (1991): 12-14.

Gustafson, James. *Ethics from a Theocentric Perspective.* Chicago: University of Chicago Press, 1981.

Halvarg, David. *The War Against the Greens: The "Wise-Use" Movement, the New Right and Anti-environmental Violence.* San Francisco: Sierra Club Books, 1994.

Hamilton, Lawrence S. "Whither the Tropical Rainforest." In *Global Perspectives in Ecology,* pp. 101-4. Edited by Thomas C. Emmel. Palo Alto, Calif.: Mayfield, 1977.

Hardin, Garrett. "Ecology and the Death of Providence." *Zygon* 15 (1980): 57-68.

_____. "The Tragedy of the Commons." *Science* 162 (1969): 1243-48.

Hermach, Tim. "The Great Tree Robbery." *The New York Times,* September 17, 1991.

Houghton, Richard A. "The Role of Forests in Affecting the Greenhouse Gas Composition of the Atmosphere." In *Global Climate Change and Life on Earth,* pp. 43-55. Edited by Richard L. Wyman. New York: Routledge, Chapman and Hall, 1991.

Houghton, Richard A., and George M. Woodwell. "Global Climatic Change," *Scientific American* 260, no. 4 (1989): 36-44.

International Union for Conservation of Nature and Natural Resources. *IUCN Red List of Threatened Animals.* Gland, Switzerland/Cambridge, U.K.: IUCN, 1990.

Jacob, Anthony T. *Acid Rain.* Madison, Wis.: Institute for Chemical Education, 1991.

Kellert, Stephen R., and Joyce K. Berry. *Phase III: Knowledge, Affection and Basic Attitudes Toward Animals in American Society.* Arlington, Va.: National Technical Information Service, 1980.

Kidner, Derek. *Genesis: An Introduction and Commentary.* Downers Grove, Ill.: InterVarsity Press, 1967.

Leopold, Aldo. *A Sand County Almanac: With Essays on Conservation from Round River.* New York: Sierra Club/Ballantine Books, 1974.

Levine, Norman D. "Roundtable: Evolution and Extinction." *BioScience* 39 (1989): 38.

Lewis, C. S. *The Abolition of Man.* New York: Macmillan, 1947.

_____. *The Great Divorce.* New York: Macmillan, 1947.

Lipske, Michael. "Who Runs America's Forests?" *National Wildlife* 28, no. 6 (1990): 24-34.

MacIntyre, Alasdair. *After Virtue.* South Bend, Ind.: Notre Dame University Press, 1981.

Marston, Ed. "Will the Bush Administration Choose Reform?" *High Country News* 33, no. 18 (1991): 13.

McHarg, Ian. *Design with Nature.* Garden City, N.Y.: Natural History Press, 1969.

Means, Richard L. "Why Worry About Nature?" *Saturday Review,* December 2,

1967.

Miller, G. Tyler, Jr. *Living in the Environment.* 7th ed. Belmont, Calif.: Wadsworth, 1992.

Monastersky, R. "Antarctic Ozone Hole Sinks to a Record Low." *Science News* 40 (1991): 244-45.

Monsma, Stephen V. *Pursuing Justice in a Sinful World.* Grand Rapids, Mich.: Eerdmans, 1984.

Montaigne. *Essays.* Trans. John Florio. New York: Everyman's Library, 1965.

Mourien, Trophime. *The Creation.* Trans. S. J. Tester. New York: Hawthorn Books, 1962.

Murphy, Elaine M. *World Population: Toward the Next Century.* Washington, D.C.: Population Reference Bureau, 1985.

Myers, Norman. *The Primary Source: Tropical Rainforests and Our Future.* New York: W. W. Norton, 1991.

_____. "Roundtable: Extinction Rates Past and Present." *BioScience* 39 (1989): 39-41.

_____. *The Sinking Ark: A New Look at the Problem of Disappearing Species.* New York: Pergamon Press, 1979.

Naisbitt, John. *Megatrends: Ten New Directions Transforming Our Lives.* New York: Warner, 1982.

Nash, James A. *Loving Nature: Ecological Integrity and Christian Responsibility.* Nashville: Abingdon, 1991.

Naveh, Zev. "Neot Kedumim." *Restoration and Management Notes* 7 (1989): 9-13.

Neuhaus, Richard John. *The Naked Public Square.* Grand Rapids, Mich.: Eerdmans, 1984.

Newby, James R., and Elizabeth S. Newby. *Between Peril and Promise.* Nashville: Thomas Nelson, 1984.

O'Brien, Joan, and Wildred Major. *In the Beginning: Creation Myths from Ancient Mesopotamia, Israel and Greece.* Chico, Calif.: Scholars Press, 1982.

O'Connor, Daniel. "Introduction: The Human and the Divine." In *Creation: The Impact of an Idea,* pp. 107-19. Edited by D. O'Connor and F. Oakley. New York: Charles Scribner's Sons, 1968.

O'Toole, Randall. "Recreation Fees and the Yellowstone Forests." In *The Greater Yellowstone Ecosystem: Redefining America's Wilderness Heritage,* pp. 41-48. Edited by Robert B. Keiter and Mark S. Boyce. New Haven, Conn.: Yale University Press, 1991.

Packer, J. I. *Knowing God.* Downers Grove, Ill.: InterVarsity Press, 1973.

Perelman, Louis J. *The Global Mind: Beyond the Limits to Growth.* New York: Mason/Charter, 1976.

Petulla, Joseph M. *American Environmental History.* San Francisco: Boyd and Fraser, 1977.

Primack, Richard B. *Essentials of Conservation Biology.* Sunderland, Mass.. Sinauer Associates, 1993.

Richards, John F. "Documenting Environmental History: Global Patterns of Land Conversion." *Environment* 26, no. 9 (1984): 6-13.

Sagan, Carl. "Guest Comment: Preserving and Cherishing the Earth—An Appeal for Joint Commitment in Science and Religion." *American Journal of Physics* 58 (1990): 615.

Sax, Joseph L. "Ecosystems and Property Rights in Greater Yellowstone: The Legal System in Transition." In *The Greater Yellowstone Ecosystem: Redefining America's Wilderness Heritage*, pp. 77-84. Edited by Robert B. Keiter and Mark S. Boyce. New Haven, Conn.: Yale University Press, 1991.

Schaeffer, Francis. *Pollution and the Death of Man: The Christian View of Ecology.* Wheaton, Ill.: Tyndale House, 1973.

Schmemann, Alexander. *For the Life of the World: Sacraments and Orthodoxy.* Crestwood, N.Y.: St. Vladimir's Seminary Press, 1973.

Schneider, Paul. "When a Whistle Blows in the Forest." *Audubon* 94, no. 1 (1992): 42-49.

Schneider, Stephen H. "The Greenhouse Effect: Science and Policy." *Science* 243 (1989): 771-81.

Schneider, Stephen H., and Penelope Boston, eds. *Scientists on Gaia.* Cambridge, Mass.: MIT Press, 1991.

Scott, J. M., B. Csuti and K. A. Smith. "Commentary: Playing Noah While Paying the Devil." *Bulletin of the Ecological Society of America* 71 (1990): 156-59.

Sessions, George, and Bill Devall. *Deep Ecology: Living As If Nature Mattered.* Salt Lake City: Gibbs M. Smith, 1985.

Shaw, James H. "Assessing the Progress Toward Leopold's Land Ethic." *Wildlife Society Bulletin* 15 (1987): 470-72.

Sheaffer, John R., and Raymond H. Brand. *Whatever Happened to Eden?* Wheaton, Ill.: Tyndale House, 1980.

Sheldon, Joseph K. *Rediscovery of Creation: A Bibliographic Study of the Church's Response to the Environmental Crisis.* Metuchen, N.J.: American Theological Library Association and Scarecrow Press, 1992.

Sider, Ronald J. *Rich Christians in an Age of Hunger.* Downers Grove, Ill.: InterVarsity Press, 1977.

Simon, Julian L., and Herman Kahn, eds. *The Resourceful Earth: A Response to Global 2000.* Oxford: Blackwell, 1984.

Sittler, Joseph. *Essays on Nature and Grace.* Philadelphia: Fortress, 1972.

Skole, David, and Compton Tucker. "Tropical Deforestation and Habitat Fragmentation in the Amazon: Data from 1978 to 1988." *Science* 260 (1993): 1905-10.

Smith, George Adam. *The Historical Geography of the Holy Land.* London: Hodder & Stoughton, 1902.

Smith, Ralph. "Old Testament Concepts of Stewardship." *Southwestern Journal of Theology* 13 (Spring 1971): 7-13.

Steinhart, Peter. "The Edge Gets Thinner." *Audubon* 85, no. 6 (1983): 94-126.

Talbot, Lee M. "Demographic Factors in Resource Depletion and Environmental Degradation in East African Rangeland." *Population and Development Review* 12 (1986): 441-51.

Tangley, Laura. "Cataloging Costa Rica's Diversity." *BioScience* 40, no. 9 (1990).

633-36.

"Two Say Politics Rule Their Agencies." *High Country News* 23, no. 18 (1991): 1, 10-12.

Udall, James R. "The Tucson Paradox." *Audubon* 87, no. 1 (1985): 98-99.

Van Dyke, Fred G. "Beyond Sand County: A Biblical Perspective on Environmental Ethics." *Journal of the American Scientific Affiliation* 37 (1985): 40-48.

Van Dyke, Fred G., Arlan J. Birkey and Ted D. Nickel. "Integration and the Christian College: Reflection on the Nineteenth Psalm." In *The Best in Theology*, 3:395-400. Edited by J. I. Packer. Carol Stream, Ill.: Christianity Today, 1989.

Von Rad, Gerhard. *Genesis: A Commentary*. Philadelphia: Westminster Press, 1961.

Wetherald, Richard T. Introduction to *Global Climate Change and Life on Earth*. Edited by Richard L. Wyman. New York: Routledge, Chapman and Hall, 1991.

White, Lynn, Jr. "The Historical Roots of Our Ecologic Crisis." *Science* 155 (March 10, 1967): 1203-7.

Wilkinson, Loren. "Global Housekeeping: Lords or Servants?" *Christianity Today* 24 (1980): 26-30.

Wilkinson, Loren, ed. *Earthkeeping: Christian Stewardship of Natural Resources*. Grand Rapids, Mich.: Eerdmans, 1980.

Wilson, Edmund O. "Threats to Biodiversity." *Scientific American* 261, no. 3 (1989): 108-18.

Wolterstorff, Nicholas. *Until Justice and Peace Embrace*. Grand Rapids, Mich.: Eerdmans, 1983.

Woodward, Kenneth. "A New Story of Creation." *Newsweek*, June 5, 1989, pp. 70-72.

Wright, John W., ed. *The Universal Almanac 1993*. Kansas City, Mo.: Andrews and McHeel, 1992.

Wright, Richard T. *Biology Through the Eyes of Faith*. San Francisco: Harper & Row, 1989.

Subject Index

acid rain, 18, 20, 114-16, 141
Adam, 59, 71, 82, 86, 90-91, 96, 98, 121
Adirondacks, 14
AIDS, 150
air pollution, 20, 127
American Forestry Congress, 14
American Journal of Physics, 195
American Lung Association, 127
American Scientific Affiliation, 10
ancient Near East, mythology, 28-30
anthropocentrism, 48, 50, 51, 76, 135-36, 182
Apostle Island National Lakeshore, 45
Aristotle, 31
Asimov, Isaac, 170
Atomic Energy Commission, 24
Atoms for Peace, 24
Au Sable Institute, 137, 168, 169
Au Sable River, 54
Baly, Dennis, 65
Barth, Karl, 85-86
Baucus, Max, 116
Beasley-Murray, G. R., 73
Behemoth, 49-50, 114
Berger, Peter, 171
Berry, Joyce, 131-32
Berry, Thomas, 81
Berry, Wendell, 43, 46, 109, 128, 140, 171
Bible, 26, 41-42, 53
biodiversity, 20, 23, 74, 112-13
biology, 26
birds, 113-14

Blackwell Forest Preserve, 24
blessing, 60-61
Blocher, Henri, 64
Bombay, 16
Bonhoeffer, Dietrich, 32, 41, 42, 46-47, 50, 66, 71, 87
Boston, Penelope, 139
Brazil, 110, 130. *See also* rainforests
Bridgewater Treatises, 182
Brueggemann, Walter, 62
Buddha, 31
Callicott, J. Baird, 181
cancer, 119, 127
capitalism, 106
carbohydrates, 20
carbon dioxide, 20-21, 22, 116-17
careerist, 168-69
Carroll, C. Ronald, 181
carrying capacity, 21, 23, 103
Carson, Rachel, 102, 103
Changes in the Land, 106
Chase, Alston, 138, 156
chlorofluorocarbons, 20, 22, 117, 119-21
Christian education, 168, 169-72, 183
Christian Environmental Association, 174
church, 100, 105, 132, 145, 148, 149, 159, 160, 170, 173, 180-81
Clean Air Act, 18, 128
Climate Institute, 118
compassion, 150-51
conservation, 42-43, 46, 107, 109
conservation biology, 26
consumption, 20, 107, 108, 119, 121, 127, 175
contemplation, 139
"continual creation," 66
control, 43
Costa Rica, 113
Cottrell, Jack, 94
covenant, 72-74, 76-77, 83,

84-88, 124
creation, 31, 50, 54; and covenant, 85-86; goodness of, 47-48; joy of, 35-36, 166-67; linkage in, 57-60, 66; and nature, 15, 39-40; ordering of, 91; redemption of, 12, 99, 123-24; as revelation, 25; usefulness of, 48-50; value of, 25-27, 46-47, 51-55
Creation Spirituality, 133
cultivation, 96, 169
Currid, John, 65
curse, 54, 64, 68, 69, 71, 72, 82
"Cyrus Principle," 133
Daly, Herman, 123
decomposition, 108, 114
Deep Ecology, 138
deforestation, 20, 110, 119, 126
deism, 33
democracy, 134, 157
Department of Energy, 24
Department of Interior, 152
Derham, William, 182
desertification, 17
developing countries, 16, 103, 150
Deward, Michigan, 106
DeWitt, Cal, 137-38
disease, 118, 150
domination, 132
Dubos, René, 45, 163-64
Dust Bowl, 109
Dustin, Daniel, 45
Earth Day, 18-19
Earthkeeping, 137
ecojustice, 105
ecologic crisis, 11
ecological religion, 178
ecology, 26, 178
economy, 43, 182
ecosystems, 19-20, 22, 111-14
Ecuador, 131-32
Eden, 53-54, 65, 96
Edwards, Jonathan, 164

About the Authors

Fred Van Dyke received his Ph.D. in environmental and forest biology from the State University of New York-Syracuse. A former wildlife research biologist with the Montana Department of Fish, Wildlife and Parks, Fred is currently assistant professor of biology at Northwestern College, Iowa, and associate professor of natural history at the Au Sable Institute of Environmental Studies in Michigan.

David Mahan received his Ph.D. in limnology from Michigan State University. He has formerly served on the faculty of Western Michigan University and as field representative for the Michigan Chapter of the Nature Conservancy. Currently Dave is associate director of the Au Sable Institute for Environmental Studies in Michigan.

Joseph Sheldon received his Ph.D. in entomology from the University of Illinois. Formerly a professor and head of the Department of Biology at Eastern College in St. Davids, Pennsylvania, Joe is now professor of biology at Messiah College, Grantham, Pennsylvania, and professor of environmental studies at the Au Sable Institute. He is the author of *Rediscovery of Creation: A Bibliographical Study of the Church's Response to the Environmental Crisis* (American Theological Library Association/Scarecrow Press, 1992) and president of the American Entomological Society.

Raymond Brand received his Ph.D. in animal ecology from the University of Michigan. He is a retired biology professor and a former chair of the Department of Biology and Division of Science at Wheaton College, Illinois. Presently Ray is a research associate of the Morton Arboretum in Lisle, Illinois. Ray is coauthor (with John R. Sheaffer) of *Whatever Happened to Eden?* (Tyndale House, 1980).